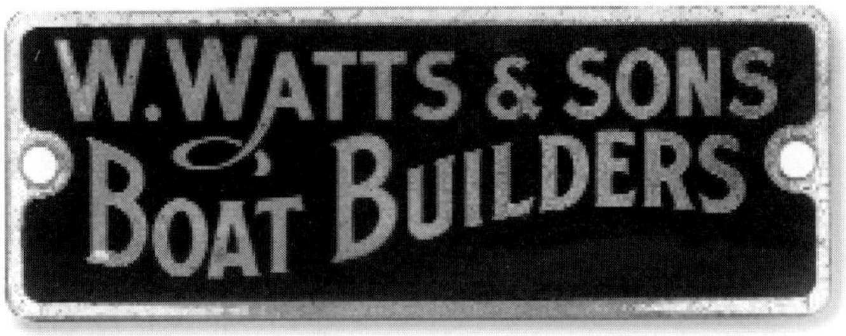
W. WATTS & SONS
BOAT BUILDERS

W. WATTS & SONS BOAT BUILDERS

CANADIAN DESIGNS FOR WORK AND PLEASURE
1842–1946

Peter Watts and Tracy Marsh

MACKINAW PRODUCTIONS

Canadian Cataloguing in Publication Data
Watts, Peter, 1957–
W. Watts & Sons, Boat Builders:
Canadian Designs for Work and Pleasure, 1842 - 1946.

Includes bibliographical references and index.

ISBN 0-9682808-0-3

1. W. Watts & Sons–History. 2. Boatbuilding–Canada-History.
I. Marsh, Tracy, 1963–   II. Title.

VM301.W38W38 1997   338.7'62382'00971   C97-901217-1

Printed and bound in Canada by Metrolitho Inc.
Sherbrooke, Quebec.

Designed by Ronald MacRae Design, Collingwood, Ontario.

Published by Mackinaw Productions
65 Beatrice Street W., Oshawa, Ontario, Canada L1G 3M7

In thanks for their support,

encouragement and understanding,

we dedicate this book to our families:

Angela, Matthew, Andrew and Laura Watts,

Brent, Janine and Anne Marsh.

"The family is like a book—the children are the leaves,
the parents are the covers that protective beauty gives.
At first the pages of the book are blank and purely fair,
But time soon writeth memories and painteth pictures there.
Love is the little golden clasp that bindeth up the trust,
Oh, break it not, lest all the leaves shall scatter and be lost."

Anonymous

W. Watts & Sons Boat Builders

CONTENTS

FOREWORD

From my earliest memories as a youngster, experimenting with unusual and wonderfully crafted hand tools in 'that old boat house', to watching my father complete his labour of love, his craft *F. C. Watts*, I knew the traditions of boat building were in my blood.

The warming wood stove in the winter months served as a comforting back drop to watch my father skillfully employ the tools and methods handed down from a century of tradition. *F. C. Watts* grew as I did. The boat progressed through the years into a beautifully constructed testament to enduring design.

The completion of this vessel was anti-climactic for my father. The finished boat would bring an end to the gathering spot, a meeting place of the great-grandsons and grandsons of Collingwood's pioneer families. The gathering of friends were as much a part of *F. C. Watts* as was the actual construction of the boat itself. In fact, the construction of the boat became secondary to the social environment that was the boat house. From listening to the tales of a distant era, to helping build a boat in the same building as my grandfather and great-grandfather, I knew the business of boat building would be an integral part of my life as well. Like a gene passed down through the centuries, my interest in boats grew steadily. My appreciation for the boat building craft grew with me through my teens and twenties. After the launch of *F. C. Watts*, my father and I were to begin a boat of wood using original molds, tools and materials. A 30' sailing craft and 14' tender would have brought the aroma of white cedar and steaming white oak back to that old boathouse.

This was not to be. It wasn't until shortly after my father's death that I had the opportunity to try my own hand at building wooden boats. I was wholly unprepared for the painstaking precision and careful applications required in designing and constructing even the simplest of craft. More fascinating yet was the ease and perfection with which my family were able to construct their boats. My experience in a fully equipped shop with close instruction and perfect working conditions, were in stark contrast to the magnificent floating accomplishments made by my family. Early on, they used only hand tools, and built by eye without diagrams to guide the construction.

Some of the most finely formed craft to ever grace our waters were constructed. I experienced in some small way the extraordinary process my family had undertaken in building vessels of every type more than a century earlier.

Many Watts built craft played a part in such early Canadian adventures as the Riel Rebellion, exploration and survey expeditions, the Klondike Gold Rush, commercial fishing and boat construction in the United States.

Today, interest in vessels built by W. Watts & Sons have earned a resurgence in interest through heritage projects, local and country wide museum displays.

My father was a fountain of information. He shared the stories with me that his father shared with him. I knew it was a story worth telling and I jumped at the opportunity to do just that.

There is nothing finer than being a part of researching, recording and retelling aspects of our great Canadian heritage.

Peter Watts, November 1997

Boats were not an important part of my world until 1985. Before that, my exposure to boats was limited to say the least. My grandfather had a little wooden motor boat at Pointe au Baril. I remember the day he let me drive for the first time. It was quite a thrill. Other than that, it was only good for frying worms on the deck before they went on the hook of the fishing rod and for going to the Station to buy more worms. There were a few other boats, but the environment around Pointe au Baril was the most memorable. Beside my Grandparent's cottage lived an unforgettable fisherman, Ben Whatley. He was building a cement fishing boat when I was still playing with dolls. He let the kids help sand the bottom of the boat, a job we soon tired of. I also spent a few nights aboard, which left me swaying like the motion of the waves until at least noon the next day.

Now, I wish I would have asked him about the boat, the boats he had before, the smoke house for fish, what kind of a living he made, how much net he used and why he moved from Thornbury to Pointe au Baril. But I didn't. Instead, I tormented bull frogs, fished for just about anything and played with dolls.

In 1985 I was hired by The Collingwood Museum. My interest in the job was to put my education to the test. I had little knowledge of anything marine. What I did have was a desire to learn all I could about the community and the people that lived there in the past. (I was born in Collingwood, but circumstance led me elsewhere as a kid.) It was about 1987 when the name Watts stuck in my mind. I knew that a man named Watts built fish boats in Collingwood, but that was about the extent of it. A little research on The Collingwood Shipyard revealed that a portion of their property was leased from one Matthew Watts. That was the second time I recall the name. The foundation was laid, I needed more information on the man who built the boats and owned a portion of the waterfront earlier than the Shipyard. As opportunity permitted, I dug deeper. The more I looked, the more fascinated I became. The interest turned into a burning passion. I don't know when it happened, but it became very important to reveal the work of Watts and tell stories about their boats, their adventures and the victory and tragedy that befalls a family that makes their living at sea. A story was coming to light about a family that built boats throughout Canada, and at key points in our Nation's history. As the country expanded west, so did they. At some point between the fascination stage and the obsession, I met Peter.

Peter, for me, symbolized the link between the past and the present. When other kids were tormenting bull frogs or playing with friends, Peter was asking questions. Thankfully, he has recalled most of the answers. I still believe that he is the link between the past and present, as far as his family is concerned. I now know him as a sentimental, generous, funny and strong willed man. He was the incentive to keep researching. In him, I saw the same ache to reveal Watts for more than just a fish boat builder beyond the shores of Collingwood. We have different perspectives, but together they are complimentary. It has been an unforgettable journey researching and compiling this book together. I thought that the completion of this book would relieve the desire to learn more about Watts and their wooden boats, but it has only added more fuel to the fire. Some day, there will be more.

Tracy Marsh, November 1997

Family of Sir Edmund Walker on board Nahma.
From the files of the late Dr. H.A.Hunter

INTRODUCTION

On shores all around the Great Lakes, experienced and novice boat builders launched boats into uncharted waters before Canada was a Nation. Many of the builders and their boats will go undocumented, forgotten by the passing of time.

When William Watts boarded a ship in Ireland to come to Upper Canada, he began a tradition of boat building that lasted for over 100 years, certainly long enough to avoid being forgotten. The company is best known in Collingwood, although their work can be traced throughout Canada. Mention Collingwood around anyone with even a passing knowledge of anything marine, steel ship building and spectacular side launches come to mind. For 103 years The Collingwood Shipyard was a part of that community, and to a certain extent, it was its identity. The wooden boats built in Collingwood deserve to be an integral part of this identity as well.

It was Watts who launched boat after boat into the bay thirty years before the Shipyard opened. He owned a portion of the waterfront property, and eventually leased parts of it to the Shipyard. During the Depression when the Shipyard wasn't employing many men, some went to work for Watts.

Still, even though they were incredibly prolific and successful as boat builders, they left a modest trail of recorded history. Much of the lack of documentation is the nature of the boat builder. They were secretive, protective, and guarded their art for only a chosen few. They were also incredibly skilled. Many boats were built by eye, an art that has all but passed away with these early craftsmen. Like the musicians who compose and never write a note, the written record of the shapes and quantities of boats were largely non-existent in the first place. These craftsmen practiced their art under the harshest of conditions, often no shelter, cold and mud. A few simple tools were all that was at hand to perform their task. Boats were sold on the faith of someone's word. Neighbours, friends and fellow fishermen and mariners paid as they could, and with what they could. One boat was shipped from Collingwood to a Doctor in the United States. The payment was a well-trained hunting dog. For a boat builder that fancied his hunt club, it was a fair trade. There is no record of the deal, only pictures of a beloved dog and the family story of the dog that was payment for a boat. This is the stuff that calls in the curious, begs you to peer just beneath the surface and see what is beyond. Once that happens, the fascination turns almost to obsession, combined with a deep sense of respect and awe of what went on before.

What does survive of the company, and the finest treasure of it's kind, is the Watts Life Boat Storage House. It served as the boat building shop for a few years in the 1940's. The boat house is a magical place. It smells of wood, grease, dust, and history. The bench is littered with nails, rivets, carriage bolts, chisels, saws, tobacco cans, and test holes from virtually every size drill imaginable. One wall sports calendars nailed on top

W. WATTS & SONS,
Boat Builders, Pine Street.

Boating is conceded by medical authorities to be among the most healthful pastimes, while everyone knows of its pleasures. A leader in this branch of industry is W. Watts & Son, builders of all kinds of boats from the light canoe to the heavy launch. This business was established fifty years ago by Mr. W. Watts, who conducted it for thirty years, and then associated with him Matthew Watts. This firm continued to do business till the death of W. Watts in 1906, when the present proprietor, Matthew Watts, took entire control, still using the old firm name of Watts & Sons. The plant has over 2,500 square feet of floor space, and a specialty is made of manufacturing metalic life boats. The trade of this concern extends throughout Canada, and is well known for the high grade products which are manufactured. These boats are universally admired as representing the acme of excellence in design, construction, finish and equipment. They are the produce of fifty years of experience in scientific boat building.

of another, on top of another. Another 3 inch spike holds receipts from Reg Watts construction of the *F. C. Watts*. A wooden jam cupboard holds various paint concoctions and varnishes used for finishing boats. Brushes hang cemented in cleaning fluid, preserved for our curious eyes today. Planks and boards run along the beams in the ceiling, many of them dating to the earlier days of the business. Some are so large they're non-existent in today's market. The pot bellied stove, surrounded by chairs of various vintages, sports a shining kettle. The scene is so inviting, it wouldn't be hard to believe that spirits gather there to continue reminiscing or telling tall tales. It's hard to resist sitting and conjuring up a tall tale just to share even if there is no one else in the building. How many times have the chairs been used to look at a boat, ponder it's progress, consider a change or admire the beauty? A gum ball machine may look a little out of place, until you hear the story about all the times the boys tried to quit smoking and took to gum chewing instead. Still, a collection of pipes hangs from a rafter.

Just high enough to be inconvenient if you really wanted one, but in constant view as a temptation and reminder that they're available if needed. A treasure indeed.

This book is to draw attention to the quantity, quality and scope of the boats built by the Watts family, and to put their work in context with the history of the development of Canada. They were a unique family, in the right place at the right time. If not for that, combined with the crucial ingredients of driving spirit, skill and hard work, we may not know about Watts and their boats today.

Compared with the thousands of boats built by Watts, this book is a beginning. It is intended as an introduction to W. Watts & Sons, and we sincerely hope that it's publication will lead to a wealth of new information. We were reminded, very early in our research, that the experts on Watts and sailing in fish boats or mackinaws, have long since passed away. Today, there are precious few who have sailed in mackinaws and can tell us of the fishermen's stories. These few are today's experts, and have given a great deal to add to our understanding of boat building, fishing and sailing. Another generation removed, we are decidedly not the experts, but the collectors of stories and pictures to help our understanding of a topic that has become a part of our every day lives over the past year.

The Project

It was over a coffee in late December of 1996 the project began. It started perhaps much like boats were sold a century ago, on a handshake and good faith. This is the foundation that has carried us through a year that neither of us could have predicted.

Some people don't believe there is such a thing as coincidence, rather that every event has a purpose or a reason. Our first meeting wasn't coincidental, but professional. Coincidental events in the years to follow meant we stayed in touch, although on a very casual basis. Great-grandson of boat builder meets Museum Curator. Meetings like that happen all the time in Museums across Canada. People who work in heritage organizations every day get to meet the descendants of the people we hope to interpret through exhibits and programmes. They share a common interest.

There were letters over the years, sharing of research victories and for each of us, a growing quest for more. In 1994, Georgian Bay held a Marine Heritage Festival. It was an opportunity to work together again. Collingwood built a replica of the Watts built *Nahma* as a volunteer project and the Collingwood Museum featured an exhibit entitled "W. Watts & Sons, Boat Builders". During the preparation for this exhibition, each of us discovered a kindred spirit.

People started hearing about Watts boats. Most of what they heard was that Watts built skiffs. Double ended, shallow draft, clinker built boats used largely in the fishing trade, and later adapted for yachting. Watts did build skiffs. Whether you call them skiffs, fish boats or mackinaws, Watts built more of them than any other kind of boat, and more than any other builder. To credit the firm of W. Watts & Sons in Canada's small craft history, we hope this book will highlight the multitude of other vessels constructed. The mackinaw was at the heart of this company. For this reason, we have adopted the term as part of our corporate identity.

We were lucky. Very lucky actually. If not for the generosity and foresight of countless individuals across Canada, this volume would simply not have been possible. Many are acknowledged in the typical fashion of a publication of this kind, but one individual needs a few more words. While still in College, a young James Barry corresponded with Captain William Watts Jr. of Vancouver. Years of letters were the foundation of Barry's published article in *Yachting Magazine*, 1940. The existence of these letters, the inquisitive nature of James Barry and Captain Watts gift of memory and story telling have given us a tremendous insight into the activities of Watts all over the Lakes, and in Vancouver. It doesn't end there. James Barry was also a source of great encouragement for us both to write what we know and continually search for more.

Writing and searching sum up 1997 very handily. Research took us to wonderful places around Canada. From backyards in Wyebridge to the shores of Coal Harbour at Vancouver, each place holds a special memory. There were even homecomings. Watts boats that were rediscovered, and a few brought home to Collingwood.

Perhaps the most exciting home coming was *Pequod*. She was a beautiful boat. Carvel, wine–glass transom and spent her very early years at the prestigious Royal Canadian Yacht Club.

When we found her, about 70 years after her construction, *Pequod* was hard to identify. Despite an improper cradle that was crushing her hull, an unsympathetic cabin addition, and a rotting keel, it was *Pequod*. Cranes, flatbeds, straps, welders, and more cradles were employed to bring her back home to the Watts Boat House. If the book never made it to press, our work was worth while when *Pequod* eased through the west doors of the Watts Boat House again. The creation of the grandfather, passed along through 'coincidence' to the grandson for restoration.

Hauling a Watts life-boat from Sault Ste Marie to Collingwood wasn't without adventure either.

Just a casual look at a Watts boat conjures up so much. The sharp, fine bow. A broad and shapely beam. Planks that are all uniform in width at the bow and stern, although they have travelled over bulging ribs along the sides and overlapped the plank before. Ribs steamed and bent at unimaginable angles. The result is a splendid, almost sensual shape that functions with perfection. Regardless of the boat style, they are the pinnacle of good design. They were beloved by those who used them. Perhaps the most amazing part in a world of prefabrication and mass production, they were made by hands. Each one was crafted as an individual boat. Each piece of wood has its own particular character. Even two planks cut from the same tree have individual characteristics. They were not only skilled builders, they had intimate knowledge of wood and it's properties.

The Watts boys didn't grow up learning how to build any boat, they learned how to build a Watts boat.

The book started out rather modest, and gradually grew to what you see now. The goal was to give Canadians the opportunity to have as much information about Watts and their boats as possible. To that end, we have tried to write for a broad audience. There are many elements to the text, therefore, some chapters are more technical by necessity than others.

Terms that may not been seen as 'politically correct' by today's language standard have been used here, like 'fisherman' and referring to boats as 'her'. This language, we felt, was appropriate for the era we have covered and for the language used by the marine community now and historically. Those individuals that fished, within the context of our work, were all men.

Finally, although we made every effort to be accurate, any error is strictly our own. We both hope that the story gives you even a portion of the pleasure we had preparing it.

Enjoy.

Next time you see a wooden boat, stop and admire the craftsmanship, imagine the hands that created it, and remember that for over one hundred years, the Watts family built some of the nicest boats around.

This Irish row boat displays a few of the classic characteristics of early Watts vessels in Canada, clinker build and double ended. This picture taken at Needles Eye, Ireland in 1912.
Photo: William James Topley, National Archives of Canada PA10814

1 FROM IRELAND TO UPPER CANADA

A NEW BEGINNING

There is a land of pure delight

Where saints immortal reign;

In-finite day excludes the night

And pleasures vanish pain.

Isaac Watts, 1674-1748

Emigration and immigration are two of the most evocative words used in any country, particularly to a nation as young as Canada. Emigration and immigration usually involve the same person simultaneously.

The reasons for emigrating from Ireland are as wide and varied as the number of people from the old sod who made the journey.

The greatest motivators for someone to leave his or her ancestral home are often invisible, to all but those who live there. Take your mind back, if you will, to a country with its origins in prehistory. Then we can begin to understand the Irish, their story, and their impassioned need to control their own destiny.

From the very origins of time when people first started to venture from their own little patch of terra firma, one goal was common: the need to create a better environment for family and loved ones. The litany of reasons that would possess a person to leave the place where ancestors, traditions and the only way of life known are virtually endless. Words cannot begin to capture the emotions that one must feel when contemplating this move, whether it be by choice or force.

How unsettling it must have been to the early citizens of Ireland to be unable to control, guide or influence even the smallest part of their lives. To many natives of Ireland the decision to leave their beloved homeland was not so much a choice, but a necessity. The Irish have been on North American soil in varying degrees, for several hundred years. One theory is that Irish monks were believed to have visited Newfoundland around the year 1000. Whatever theory or hypothesis subscribed to, it can safely be said the influence of the Irish people has been with Canadians for a great number of years.

The story of William Watts and his family begins near the end of the Napoleonic Wars, circa 1815. It was a period when William Watts' family was witness to many

William Watts Sr. in 1884.
Collingwood
Museum Collection

changes stemming from the ending of political and economic encumbrances caused by the rule of Napoleon. In largely agricultural, backward Ireland, falling prices for farm produce, absentee landlordism and over-population resulted in widespread and severe poverty. Such was the magnitude of Ireland's over-population, that in 1815, some 6 million Irish struggled to survive on approximately 13 million acres of land, farmed by the most archaic and antiquated methods.

In fact, it was from of the most densely populated areas of Ireland, Ulster and the adjoining counties of North Connaught and North Leimster, that the vast majority of Irish immigrants to Canada originated. For the most part they were farmers and weavers seeking to better their prospects overseas, after facing a depressed market for agricultural products and a structural reorganization of the Irish linen industry.

Socio-economic conditions over the face of Europe were, in a word, abysmal. "In the early 1800's, Ireland was even worse off. The political scene was unstable, counties at loggerheads with other counties right down to neighbourhood skirmishes and open confrontation, with its own citizens taking the brunt of this upheaval. Simply because there was no way to fight what they could not see, the makers of Irish rules were THE BRITISH." [1]

In an attempt to quiet this brewing rebellion, the British Parliament decided it would assist Irish settlers across the Atlantic under the watchful eye of Peter Robinson. Hence two instant settlements for Upper

---

1. Knowles, Valerie. *Strangers at our Gates*, Dundurn Press 1992

COUNTY MAP OF IRELAND

.... Boundary of Northern Ireland

Canada, one being in the Peterborough area, and the other in Perth Township area, all c. 1825.

The British in 1827 decided this type of peace keeping for the Irish was too expensive, but by the time the funding was cut, the news of the success of these emigrants from the Emerald Isle started an outpouring of people that would not subside for many years. From 1830 to 1840, thousands upon thousands of families left not only Ireland, but the whole of Great Britain and Europe.

It is at this point Matthew and William Watts prepared for their journey to the new land. The legendary potato famine of the 1840's caused thousands to starve and suffer horrendously. However, this was not the case for the young Watts family. The Watts brothers of the 1840's were already experienced craftsmen, plying their trade on the shores of Sligo County, Ireland. All the factors which precipitated that move may never be fully known. What we do know is that the journey was made to the new world and the historic influences on the Canadas had begun.

The mere thought of being your own boss and having control of your own destiny are only two factors that would assist Matthew and William in the decision to leave family, home and country. Matthew and William were fortunate enough to escape disease and many of the insurmountable horrors so many of their countrymen succumbed to on their voyage to North America. So atrocious were the conditions on the voyages, the vessels earned the morbid name coffin ships. The six-to-eight week voyages seemed an eternity for most, and ended in eternity for the less fortunate.

No light, no sanitation, diseases of every manner were present. Whatever inhumanities were encountered on these voyages, they paled in comparison to the country–wide state of decay at home. An Ireland first invaded in 1169, and for the next several hundred years, unwilling to concede or be absorbed by the mighty British Empire, made the Emerald Isle a powder keg waiting for the proper spark. Emigration seemed to be a solution for the British and allowed steam to be released in the form of people, quite possibly averting future untold hardship.

Matthew and William sailed from known to unknown, and while not aware of it at the time, the brothers were in the process of laying the groundwork for their future in their new home of Canada. The sheer nature of the whole Irish experience helped to hone character, strength, will and resolve. This placed a family on Canada's shores that would succeed in the forbidding and untamed lands.

Most emigrants from Ireland landed on Grosse Île in the St. Lawrence, just off Montreal. This is the first sight many would have in the new land.

"The voyage might take one month, or four, if the ship was not shipwrecked or sunk on the way. Emigrant families crossed the ocean packed together in dark, airless holds with their belongings crammed in around them. They were just another cargo for the sea captains who hauled timber to Britain on the return voyage. The most terrifying danger was cholera, a disease that rampaged through Europe and North America in the 1830's. The victims suffered sudden, violent cramps, diarrhea, and vomiting.

Usually cholera victims died in a few hours, but some people carried the disease without getting sick. The colonies tried desperately to keep cholera out. Lower Canada made Grosse Île a quarantine station for immigrant ships coming up the St. Lawrence. The immigrants were eager to start their lives in Canada, and they were desperate to escape the cramped, stinking ships. But first, any who showed signs of sickness, had to go ashore to Grosse Isles quarantine sheds. They stayed there until they recovered, or died." [2]

Such was the typical scene to greet newcomers to our shores. Many thousands venturing no farther rest in mass graves on the Island. These conditions magnified exponentially as the flow of Irish doubled, tripled and quadrupled over the next few decades. Although the exact year Matthew and William's venture from their Irish home on the shores of Sligo County is not known, it was most likely just prior to 1843. The two young brothers eventually made their way to the Island just off the shores of Muddy York, the future city of Toronto.

Jane Watts, older sister of the two, born February 25, 1819, took the journey in 1843 at the age of 24. [3] It was a crossing which took six weeks and 3 days, jammed in a vessel with 500 other passengers.

The quest for the new land had finally been realized. Now it was time for the task at hand, to establish a livelihood as boat builders. The next several years were spent doing just that. Boats for a new country, to feed the demand of a growing Dominion.

Jane (Watts) Bishop. George Akitt Collection

2. Lunn & Moore. *The Story of Canada*, Leister Publishing, Toronto 1992
3. The Collingwood Bulletin, *Pioneer Lady Called Away*, April 17, 1913

2 TORONTO ISLAND

THE LONELY LITTLE OUTCROPPING

For a moment of night
we have a glimpse of ourselves
and our world islanded
in its stream of stars—pilgrims
of mortality, voyaging between
horizons across the eternal seas
of space and time.

Henry Beston, 1888-1968
The Outermost House

The political and economic factors that forged the skills and character of William Watts in his Irish home are the same factors and elements that continued his drive in the untamed, untried Canada. Landing at ports in Quebec meant immigrants were finally free to breathe the fresh air of a new and virtually bountiless land. Mortal folks felt immortal.

Matthew and William pushed on to Toronto, and in particular, Toronto Island. "When we arrived, there were but two other shanties besides ours,"[1] recalled their sister Jane.

Toronto Island, the lonely little outcropping on Lake Ontario, was not of much value or concern, merely a breakwater for Muddy York. Lonely outcropping or not, this is where it was all to begin for Jane, Matthew and William. To build with a few simple hand tools and possessions swept away from the old sod, a boat building legacy was born that still influences us today. The first recorded craft built by the brothers was a clinker–built sailboat. William Watts Jr., son of William notes: "I believe he built the first one in Canada on Toronto Island for one David Ward, then lightkeeper."[2] It would be the first of many boats on the island, and the first in a long line of craft for light keepers.

From the time of their arrival, survival by one's wits in the early days was the norm rather than the exception. Quiet rumblings of a rail line persisted. Not just any rail line, but a rail line that would be a direct route from the lower lakes to a yet–to–be determined spot on Georgian Bay. This would open up trade, both to and from the western and northern areas of this immense country. From the mere conception of this route, it was guised in politics and banter from private enterprise,

1. The Collingwood Bulletin, *Pioneer Lady Called Away*, April 17, 1913
2. Captain William Watts Jr. to James Barry, September 8, 1939

7

as to who would build it and where the terminus would be — the latter being the most important.

Early Toronto was home to a number of powerful and influential Irish. These powers ebbed and flowed, as always, when immigration and political instability are at the forefront. Talk of the pending railway line was a hot topic for Toronto newspapers. Businessmen and entrepreneurs discussed the impact this decision would have on their commercial enterprises. Suitably informed, William, after construction of a number and variety of craft on Toronto Island, began his trek north from Muddy York.

This undertaking was on foot through a combination of military trails, native trade routes, river banks and swamps. The journey lasted weeks. Matthew managed the boat building business on his own. Family history indicates William made at least two journeys by foot to the Nottawasaga Bay area, both in the late 1840's. The third time he stayed. With a business established and producing on Toronto Island, William could not afford to waste any time scouting the area of Collingwood. The route west, as it was commonly called, can be traced back to a military function in its infancy. Lieutenant-Colonel John Graves Simcoe made attempts to survey and carve out a route that would serve as a military short cut, helping to keep our southern neighbours at arm's length.

"Inspired by the stories that he had heard about a trail connecting his newly created York with Lake Huron, Simcoe set out from the mouth of the Humber River on the 25th of September 1793 to follow a route to Machedash Bay." [3]

David Ward's home, Toronto Island. Watercolour.: A.D. Patterson.
Royal Ontario Museum.

So the trail was blazed, and the dies were set. Simcoe called it Glouchester, now known as Penetanguishene. In the winter these routes were almost as impassable as they were in spring and summer. Summer was a series of bug–infested swamps, rough, uncharted lakes, and unnavigatable

3. Berchem, F. R. *The Yonge Street Story*, National Heritage/Natural Historic Inc. 1996

streams and rivers. In winter, extreme cold and snow made even walking an arduous task.

The foundation to make it possible to even discuss the establishment of a rail line can be traced to 1785, when the Treaty of Paris was signed. The Treaty was between the United States and Britain, which delivered the south shore of the Great Lakes into American hands. This put all major trade routes clearly in American territory. At once it could be seen that an alternate route was needed, as the old Toronto portage was a vital link with the west. Using military labour, Simcoe began the huge task of carving a route through to Lake Simcoe, then on by water courses through to Georgian Bay to connect with the west. Hence a port for shipping was established on the shores of Georgian Bay. The following excerpt gives a colourful view of the route west:

from Kempenfeldt to Penetanguishene. The case for Penetanguishene, which Simcoe had once proposed, would now be advocated with increasing urgency in the alarm following the British disaster on Lake Erie. Lord Bathurst, secretary of state, instructed Prevost in a dispatch of 3rd of December 1813 to proceed with the defenses

Toronto Harbour. A. Jamieson. Royal Ontario Museum.

"Should our fleet be totally destroyed on Lake Erie, as we have reason to believe, the bay at Machedash or Penetanguishene are both good harbours and there is plenty of excellent wood in the vicinity for constructing a vessel of any dimensions. And on the 23rd of October, he forwarded to Freer a map of Lake Simcoe on a large scale. I think that if a road is to be cut, the best route is

necessary to combat the American threat to Lake Huron. Even Prevost seems to have been pricked into an awareness that things were looking pretty grim and must have been relieved when Lieutenant–General Drummond reported back to him on 19th of January 1814, "I beg to assure you that I have lost no time in giving ample instructions relating to the supply of troops and provisions to be forwarded to Michilimackinac by Lake Simcoe and Huron, and also with regard to the building of gun boats and batteaux at Panatang (sic) for their conveyance thither.

A little more than a week later, and Drummond provided further details hedged about with reservations from the authority of several credible persons and likewise for Mr. Wilmot, the surveyor, who had been employed in running the line from Lake Simcoe to Penitangiushan (sic) Bay, that it is impracticable to transport anything by that route previous to a road being cut upwards of 30 miles in length, and that it was calculated to take 200 men for at least 3 weeks before it could be made passable, and in case of deep snow it could not be done at all. In consequence of the delay, in difficulty attending such a measure, Mr. Cruickshanks has made arrangements for forwarding supplies to Nottawasaga Bay on Lake Huron, a distance of only 20 miles from Penitangiushan (sic). The opening of the road to the river, leading to Nottawasaga Bay will take but 12 men for about 10 days and in the course of a few days, as soon as a shed can be erected on the other side of Lake Simcoe he will commence sending the stores across it, should a thaw not prevent. This mode of proceeding would undoubtedly prove somewhat expensive, but I see no alternative. Some sort of extension had to be pushed through from Yonge Street, but it was not going to be easy and time had run out." [4]

As the passage illustrates, as early as the 1780's a route north and west was not only of economic importance, but

---

4. Berchem, F. R. *The Yonge Street Story*,
   National Heritage/Natural History Inc. 1996

was just as important strategically as the fledgling Upper and Lower Canadas attempted to exert their control over this vast area. The view also foreshadowed some facts that would come to the forefront, as hostilities settled between the United States and Canada. The opportunity of trade and commerce would pull the attention of a fireplug of an Irishman, William Watts, toward Georgian Bay.

The vast wealth and virgin timber, and fish lay virtually untapped commercially. Yonge Street and the route west via Georgian Bay shared much of the same interests militarily and economically. With the dawn of the 19th century creeping closer, the economic and transportation needs certainly gave each route their own separate but equally important lines of growth and development. The 1820's and 1830's still saw Toronto in constant friction with the United States. A depressed economy pervaded the whole of Upper Canada in this time period. Be that as it may, the Toronto area began to see a slight glimmer of hope by the very late 1830's. In 1839, the coupling of Upper and Lower Canada into a cohesive body precipitated other progress essential to the growth and development of a St. Lawrence Seaway system. Parallel to Canada's economic recovery, the European countries started to rebound from a severe recession. This was all good news for the Canadas. Toronto at this time was established as a trade, economic and social centre that was not to be relinquished. Even the making of Kingston as the capital city, while it caused severe protests in news copy, never caused Toronto to look back economically. With this boom, Toronto could now capitalize on its situation and develop its rail service and become a major shipping terminus. This period in the 1840's was when the Watts family set down their firm foundations. At that time, the sky was the limit for their entrepreneurial spirit.

Opportunities were around every corner, whether in the city or in the direction of a proposed railway line. With the luck of the Irish, or through the eyes of shrewd businessmen, Matthew and William preceded the railway's progress to venture into the area of Georgian Bay at the future site of Collingwood.

In the early 1850's, William was fishing and building boats on the shore of Georgian Bay and had a number of men in his employ.

The populace in Toronto was demanding railway lines. The roads up to this time were stump–infested sink holes, festooned with all manner of discomforts, waiting to halt travel for extended periods. Even the winter months proved daunting and treacherous. Fast flowing streams that never completely froze over, drifting snow that was impossible to wade through and the constant thaw and freeze made any kind of crude trail a feat of engineering to navigate.

Time was becoming a factor and roads could not be counted on, so talk turned to trains. The signing of the Reciprocity Treaty of 1854 brought free trade on timber, grain and other items that Canadians were growing and cutting. With the Reciprocity Treaty, Canadians now had a direct link across the lake with a major trading partner and large world consumer, the United States. An opening for ease of shipment to Europe without fear of freeze up,

the future of rail to Georgian Bay would tap the untold wealth of the west and the upper Great Lakes. A report from a Rail Road engineer who surveyed the Toronto to Lake Huron route wrote as follows:

"The Toronto and Lake Huron railroad, would attract from our neighbours a large share of the carrying trade at present almost entirely monopolized by the Hudson and Erie Canal cannot be doubted. The railroad between Boston and Albanee will bring former into the same route as New York and should be constructed, it would be another feeder to Toronto and Lake Huron railway. When the improvements of the St. Lawrence are completed, the trade to and from the route will still be more drawn in our direction and in that of the railway in question.
The Patriot, March 31, 1837

So in effect, the railway to Nottawasaga Bay on the southern shores of Georgian Bay would make a connection fast, time–efficient and effective, linking the upper lakes. This economic dream, which was given thought in the late 1700's, planned in the 1840's finally got working in the 1850's. The offshoot to all of this was the opening of vast agricultural areas along the train routes, which were significant in cultural as well as economic veins. Long after the political banter was over, Collingwood rose from the dust as the terminus of the rail line from Toronto to the shores of mighty Georgian Bay.

What was left was the task of laying the rails and driving for Collingwood. And drive they did. The rail lines reached Collingwood in 1855. The succeeding years would make Collingwood a boom town, the "Chicago of the North" as it was optimistically named. Massive interconnecting shipping schedules focused on Chicago, Sault Ste. Marie and the west of Canada. There were over 2,000 permanent residents by 1857. Even neighbouring shore towns and villages were drawn to ship from Collingwood.

The rail line proved just plain business sense. The Ontario, Simcoe & Huron had turned Georgian Bay wild lands into a thriving town. What Matthew and William Watts had here were the makings of success. The first commercial enterprise in the area, and the first employer, made his unforgettable and immense mark both in Collingwood and nation wide. Matthew and William commercially fished and built boats for their own use,

and retailed a number to those wanting to make a living in the fish trade.

With just a few basic hand tools, at the mercy of the elements and nature, finely–formed vessels were created from a standing timber. These vessels were a lifeline of food and transportation. Without the boats, there was no livelihood. William would grow and prosper building all manner of craft, barges, schooners, life boats, and scows with fish boats being the main stay of the business. Other craft were built as demanded for more specialized marine uses. Cargo, timber transport, passengers and dry goods all had to be moved. With a head start on the railroad, the Watts boat building company was already clearly established by the time the Northern pushed through.

William Watts carried this saw with him from Toronto Island to Georgian Bay.
Watts Collection

Fishing shacks at Collingwood, 1870
Collingwood Museum Collection X973.582.1

3 HEN & CHICKENS HARBOUR

DENSE FOREST OF THE WILDEST SORT

Destiny is not a matter

of chance, it is a matter

of choice, it is not a thing

to be waited for,

it is a thing to be achieved.

W. J. Bryan–speech 1899

"**A** dense forest of the wildest sort," is how Fred Hodgson, an early Collingwood settler, described the region in the early 1850's. Hodgson, a poetic author and architect, aptly illustrates the natural beauty, magnified by the still–untamed forest and the life within it. For a boat builder, the spectrum of available lumber in proximity to the silvery waters of Georgian Bay was a natural advantage. This, sweetened by the promise of the terminus to the Northern Railway, would provide an unparalleled opportunity. It was called Hen & Chickens by the mariners who used the harbour for shelter. It took its name from a large island surrounded by a series of smaller ones at the mouth of the harbour. The name stuck, for a time at least.

A formidable sum of $300,000 was requested of Simcoe County Council in the early 1850's by the Railway Company. If the support was forthcoming, the Northern Railway would have the financial backing to build a portage route between Lake Ontario and Lake Huron. The farmers were strongly opposed to such an absurd sum of money for the railway. In a gutsy and visionary move, the vote was cast in support, and the terminus for the railway was to be decided. It was Peter Ferguson who broke a tie vote in favour of the road. He voted against the wishes of his father, his family and all of his friends. Most taxpayers feared the huge expense would cause them to lose their farms they had worked so hard to develop. Ferguson was a particularly well educated man in his time. His expertise gained him the position of Reeve, postmaster, school teacher and store keeper at the nearby village of Duntroon. For all his accomplishments, Ferguson will be remembered as the man who brought the railway to Georgian Bay.

The port for the line had to be accessible and large enough for modern lake-going passenger vessels. Another consideration was the grade of the land. Too steep an incline meant engines had to work harder, burn more wood and take longer en route. Penetanguishene was an option, but the grade rose 60 feet to the

Above: *An artist's rendering of Collingwood Harbour, May 1854.*
The only activity along the shore, besides a few boats, are a group of
surveyors– likely from the railway.
Collingwood Museum Collection X976.615.1

Collingwood in the 1850's was a vast unpopulated swampland, until
the railway came to town. Along this wild shore, a double-masted fish
boat sets sail. Collingwood Museum Collection X969.583.1

16

mile. The Collingwood route was not the shortest, but Fred Cumberland, chief engineer for the railroad argued "the Collingwood line skirting or passing through the Townships of Vespra, Essa, Tosorontio, Sunnidale and Nottawasaga, offers far greater inducements for the location of the line, than the country northeast of Barrie; for even were the extent and fertility of both sections equal in value as in relation to the road, it is evident that the southern limits of the eastern tract are connected by Lake Simcoe, and the northern by Gloucester and Nottawasaga Bays with your Railroad. Their trade will still be beneficially served and to a great extent secured to the line, on the adoption of the Collingwood route; whilst were that to Penetanguishene selected, all these fertile Townships to the west would fail in obtaining an outlet..."

Seemingly, Hen & Chickens Harbour was an inappropriate name for the terminus of the most important rail line in the Dominion. In order to give the region a more majestic name, a few of the locals are reported to have taken a bottle of moonshine out into the harbour and listed names of British Admiralty. Lord Admiral Cuthbert Collingwood emerged the winner, even though he had no connections to the area.

Watts and any other industrious settler had ample notice that a rail route was desired from Toronto to Georgian Bay. Even prior to their arrival at Toronto Island around 1843, there had already been one attempt to put an Act through the Legislature to construct the Northern Railroad. There were a total of three attempts to make the dream a reality: once in 1836, again in 1845 and finally a successful bid in 1849.

Promotion for the site of the terminus was overwhelming. It was to be a boom town. It was to be "Chicago of the North." In fact, in the early 1850's the only cleared street was along the waterfront, originally known as Front Street (now First Street). The main street, called Hurontario (as it ran from Lake Huron to Lake Ontario), was only partly cleared with a few stumps lining the road. It truly was little more than a swamp, even as late as 1850. Only a modest wind would blow water from the lake into homes and businesses. The bulk of the enterprise in the town was comprised of saloons, soon to be replaced by hotels with the arrival of the railway.

Watts wasn't the only one who had the vision to capitalize on the promise of the rail line. Joel Underwood, who owned 335 acres of the town now known as Collingwood, secured 3 partners to erect a steam saw mill on the site. One was Benjamin W. Smith, Sheriff of Simcoe County. With Smith's privileged position on County Council, he clearly had insight that Collingwood was most likely to be selected as the terminus. He didn't hesitate to form a partnership with Underwood, and promptly moved his residence to Collingwood as well. The Mill was completed two years before the railway.

The Watts family arrived on Collingwood's shore in 1850. By the winter of 1853, William had a few men employed in boat building. That winter was viciously cold. Only a handful of families stayed put. At a time when William Watts was reported to have "a few men working for him,"[1] the railway only saw fit to have one agent. There was the saw-miller and the staff of the tavern and boarding house, and few other neighbours to speak

1. Belden Atlas of Simcoe County, 1883

of. Watts' fishing savvy became a survival skill. The only food to nourish the village for three weeks was bread and fish. Quite a spread for the place that would be the terminus for the railway.

Lumber was a major industry around the whole of Georgian Bay. Collingwood was no exception. In the early days of William's and Matthew's arrival, the trees were plentiful, varied and massive. A series of street names in Collingwood are a reminder of the assortment and quantity of lumber that was native to the area. Pine, Maple, Beech, Birch, Oak, Cedar, Walnut, Hickory and Spruce Streets form the nucleus of the western residential section of town. In this abundant place, brothers William and Matthew felled trees where they grew, and turned them into sleek fishing boats. The vast wealth of virgin timber and fish lay virtually untapped commercially. Simcoe County was noted for their pristine stock of tall trees. The British reportedly sent naval scouts to bring back tall pines for masts on iron ships, an impossible task before the arrival of the railway.

Fishermen couldn't take away as much fish as the Bay had to offer. Whitefish, Lake Trout, Pickerel, Herring and Sturgeon formed the backbone of the industry, and there were plenty of them. Georgian Bay fishermen started using gill nets around 1834. [2] Gill nets were made of cotton and linen about six feet in height, and in varying lengths. The top line was lined with cork for flotation, and the bottom with leads. Nets were dropped and picked up the next day, usually teaming with Whitefish and Lake Trout.

For William and Matthew, the conditions couldn't have been better. The lumber was all around, all they had to do was go and get it. The fishing industry had not yet peaked, and there was no shortage of would-be fishermen wanting boats to head up the lake to the fishing grounds.

The first commercial Watts operation was just west of the junction of Hurontario Street and the waterfront. The shore line in the 1850's was substantially different than what exists today. The water's edge in 1850 was a few hundred feet south of its current location. From the doors of the boat shop, boats were simply launched into the water. One after another, double-ended wooden fish boats splashed into Georgian Bay, crafted by William & Matthew Watts.

As fishing flourished, an increasing number of schooners called at Collingwood harbour to take salted barrels of fish south to the markets. Shallow waters prevented the larger vessels from coming too close to shore. This geographic short–coming was simply another bonus for the Watts boat shop. Boats were needed to take the catch out to moored schooners, and act as escort in and out of the harbour.

Business was successful and the Watts brothers earned a reputation as excellent and prolific boat builders. At a time when opportunities for shipping boats by rail was expanding, William left Collingwood and returned to Ireland.

In Ireland, William married Susan Newton at Kilglass parish, County Sligo, in 1857. Susan's father Thomas was a sea captain. The wedding took place June 30. Across the Atlantic in Collingwood, Matthew operated the business again in the absence of his younger brother. It is uncertain if William stayed for any length of time in Ireland, or returned in short order to Collingwood.

2. Report of the Georgian Bay Fisheries Commission,
   PAC RG 23, Volume 388 File 3567 part 1

Family oral traditions note that William and Susan had a strong desire to give each of their children an Irish birthplace, and it is reported that Susan travelled back to the old country to give birth to a number of their children. By the spring of 1858, their first child was born, a son. In a practice steeped in tradition, William and Susan named him Matthew. Matthew was born in Macduff, County Sligo in Ireland, followed by Miriam, who was born in December of 1860. It is not known if William accompanied her on these voyages back to Ireland, but it is an indication of the level of financial comfort they were enjoying by this time.

While William was establishing a family in Ireland, Matthew and Jane were doing the same in Collingwood. Matthew and Farlina Watts had three sons, each born in Collingwood. The first born was named William, the second Matthew and then James. Jane Watts married an Irish-born fisherman named William Bishop. Their first son was named Robert William, their second was Matthew.

William retained his position as head of the company upon his return from Ireland. In Collingwood, his family began to grow, rounding out to 14 children in total. The crew at the boat yard was growing in number and expertise. Matthew Walton was one of the earlier members of the staff who was not a family member. Walton was tall and rugged but quiet in personality. His primary function was sail maker. On recreational fishing and hunting trips, Matthew Walton was taken along as the cook.

William, Matthew and Jane Watts had found their way to a land that offered materials, products and customers, and with the railway an opportunity for expansion of incredible proportions. What would happen to the little hollow called Hen & Chickens Harbour in the ensuing years would alter the fortune of many citizens. The arrival of the Northern Railway at Collingwood was the pivotal point for the community. Many credit the industry of Shipbuilding as the catalyst for building the town. While Shipbuilding was vitally important, it was established because of the connection by rail. The Toronto *Globe* gave credit to the importance of the railway by noting:

"Ontario may fairly claim the credit of having taken the initiative in Canadian railway construction, for, with the exception of an inconsequential line in the Province of Quebec, the Ontario, Simcoe & Huron Railway – named after the three lakes on which were its chief objective points - was the first railway in the Dominion opened for passenger and freight traffic." Feb. 22, 1890.

This being the case, the Watts', along with other spirited settlers, can fairly claim credit for taking full advantage of a Dominion on the verge of expansion. As soon as the steam locomotive named *Lady Elgin* steamed into town, Hen & Chickens Island began to transform into 'Chicago of the North.'

A detailed engraving of Collingwood early shore by E.L. Field
Collingwood Museum Collection

HEN & CHICKENS HARBOUR

The Terminus of the Northern Road of Collingwood's new rail station, 1855. This station sat parallel to Front Street. The engines pass right through massive arches. The station burnt in the 1870's.
Collingwood Museum Collection

4 COMING OF AGE

THE TRUE CHICAGO OF THE NORTH

At half-past one on New Year's Day 1855, Engine No. 1 steamed into Collingwood's impressive new Railway station. The *Lady Elgin* would be the symbol for dramatic change on Georgian Bay. It was the completion of a five-hour journey from Toronto and at least a decade in planning. The *Northern Advance* reported on January 10, 1855:

"This is a scale of travel which cannot be excelled in any part of Europe or America, and accomplished, in this instance, without the slightest inconvenience or accident."

Collingwood was catapulted into the modern era. It was incorporated as a town without ever having been a village. Settlers began to flock to the town and pieces of sub-standard property were sold for $1,000, when they were virtually worthless a few years before.

Engine No. 1, Lady Elgin, *the first to steam into Collingwood, January 1, 1855. John Harvie, pictured near the cow catcher, was the conductor.*
Collingwood Museum Collection.

Farmers could now market their crops along the 95-mile rail line, rather than to the small local market. Access to manufactured goods was now affordable. Before the railway, prices were too exorbitant for the great majority of people. The impact on commercial enterprise was clear. The *Northern Advance* noted:

"In all of the varied and extensive operations of life, whatever be their nature,

The Hotchkiss & Peckham Sawmill was constructed c. 1870. It was later sold to A.M. Dodge. Note the proximity to the Watts boat yard and the production of boats.
Collingwood
Museum Collection

Employees of the Hotchkiss & Peckham Sawmill, Collingwood.
Collingwood
Museum Collection

and wheresoever performed, profit is the object. If that profit can be increased and realized by the introduction and adoption of any new method or principle by which those operations can be more efficiently and more satisfactorily effected, where, we would ask, is the man who would shut his eyes to the prospect of advancing his own interest by the adoption and use of facilities, created and brought into operation by genuine talent and industry? By these combined elements of the mind, railways have been created and established." *January 10, 1855*

Newspapers, hotels and churches began. Rev. E. Sallows, who had established a mission at Collingwood, made these observations in 1855:

"Nearly, if not all the land is taken up in the surrounding townships; the people are flocking in from various parts; and go where you will, all are hard at work, and improvements are being made. Villages are springing up along the railroad track, and other places where congregations are collected, and numbers listen with devout attention to the 'glad tidings of great joy' perhaps no place in Canada ever made such rapid progress in so short a time." [1]

Only a year before, Rev. Sallows said, "the country is at present thinly settled and appointments are far distant from each other."

The Watts family were members of All Saints Anglican

---

1. Rev. E. Sallows : Report on Collingwood Harbour 1854-55.
   Archives of Victoria College

Church as soon as a congregation was established in 1855. Jane (Watts) Bishop was instrumental in the organization and construction of a new church in Collingwood's east end, St. Timothy's. Many worship services were held in her home. William acted as Chief

Members of the elite Blackstone Hunt Club show off the results of their annual trip. Wm. Watts Sr. is kneeling in the front row far right, Matthew Watts is standing, third from left. Matthew Walton, sailmaker at the boat shop, is pictured in the white apron.
Collingwood Museum Collection.

Constable in the early Collingwood Police Force. He took frequent leaves of absence in three month durations to tend to his business.

William and his son Matthew were charter members of the elite Blackstone Hunt Club. This exclusive group launched annual pilgrimages to hunt the wildlife of

Collingwood,_____ 189

This Certifies that I have hired of WILLIAM WATTS, of the Town of Collingwood,
ONE FISHING BOAT

(and rigging belonging to it) upon the following terms :

I paid this day   Dollars, and agree to pay promptly at the
office of the said WILLIAM WATTS, Collingwood, Ont., when the same becomes due, without
any demand to be made therefor, the further sum of
Dollars, as follows,

On the	day of	189 ,		Dollars,
On the	day of	189 ,		Dollars,
On the	day of	189 ,		Dollars,
On the	day of	189 ,		Dollars,

And it is expressly understood that until the whole sum of
Dollars is paid, the said WILLIAM WATTS, neither parts with, nor do I acquire any title to the said Fishing Boat, and in case of failure to pay any of the said amounts above stated within the time aforesaid, I do hereby authorize the said WILLIAM WATTS, or any of his authorized Agents, to enter upon and remove said Fishing Boat and rigging wherever the same may be found.

I also Agree not to remove, or take away from the Georgian Bay, the said Fishing Boat and rigging from   without the written consent of the said WILLIAM WATTS

P. O. Address :

_____

_____

Residence,_____

_____

Witness,_____

NO CREDIT allowed on these Leases unless payments are made at the Office of WILLIAM WATTS, or to parties receive or receipt for the same.

Lease agreement for the temporary use of a Watts fish boat. Watts Collection.

A variety of small craft were offered for lease at W. Watts & Sons. This was taken summer, 1887.
Collingwood Museum Collection.

northern Georgian Bay. Only members who could escape the incredible scrutiny of the existing club members needed apply.

Other Watts children, like Daisy and Tom, were a part of the growing drama scene. Fine theatrical presentations were held regularly at the well-appointed Opera House, on the second floor of the Town Hall. William joined the Masonic Lodge, where he remained a member for life.

Fishing grew at an enormous rate. Any photograph of Collingwood harbour at this time invariably shows the fishing fleet. These fish boats, as they were called, were the largest fleet of craft on the lakes. According to a report on the commission of Georgian Bay fisheries, 2,346,800 pounds of whitefish were taken out of the bay in 1875. As their letterhead proclaims, the firm of W. Watts & Sons was producing a variety of craft and in remarkable quantity. Leases of double-ended fish boats of varying sizes were added to the company's list of services. Around twenty-five boats were maintained by Watts and were leased for whatever period the customer desired. Fishermen starting a new business, or just wanting to try their hand, had an opportunity to rent a boat completely outfitted with nets and boxes. With the growing demand for a variety of boats, the trades in the shop became more specialized. Watts employed tinsmiths, blacksmiths, riggers and a sail maker. Estimates of the number of men he had on staff during this time vary. At the least it was ten and may have been as many as twenty.

Veteran Collingwood fishermen, Art and Brian Drever,

report the first fishing license in their family was granted in 1885. "In the old days, when you got a license, the license said north of Collingwood. Any place north of Collingwood, as long as you were in Georgian Bay, you could fish." Although there was little if any monitoring of the fishing licenses, nobody went beyond Georgian Bay out of Collingwood. The Drevers had fish boats built by Watts. "I'd say 80% of the fish boats in Georgian Bay were built by the Watts boat works here in Collingwood. And they'd go up and fish, whether it would be in Killarney or where ever," noted Brian Drever. When the Drever family switched to larger fish tugs, they still had a Watts built life boat hanging from the davits. Recalling the routes of Collingwood fishermen, William Watts Jr. reports:

"Now the Collingwood boats left at different periods, some going to North Shore, some to Squaw Island, some to Killarney, some to the Duck Islands, some to Detour and many to Lake Superior at various stations. And they generally followed the ice, some times got caught in it and they struggled back at different periods. Some came home iced to the mast heads as late as December 15." [2]

When two Collingwood men discovered a rich fishing ground in the middle of Lake Superior, four Collingwood fish boats were delivered to haul in the catch.

Lorne Joyce, early fishing historian and descendent of a commercial fishing family in Bronte, proclaims that the

2. Captain William Watts Jr. to James Barry, January 12, 1939.

Due to the increase in all kinds of marine activity, boats were being constructed anywhere along the shoreline. Note the small white tug nearing completion on the breakwall. Collingwood Museum Collection

This view of the slip at the Collingwood Shipyard shows W. Watts & Sons early location on the east side of the slip (identified by the number 2). The shop was later floated to a location just west of the slip. Collingwood Museum Collection

"largest Canadian fish-boat builders were the Watts of Collingwood." [3]

Lighthouse keepers from around the Lakes had a Watts-built tender. They were the only way of getting on and off the light. In late December, when some keepers left for home, small wooden lapstrake tenders were the only thing separating the keepers and their families from ice–filled, frigid waters. Jim Keith, former light keeper for the Western Islands recalls his own Watts built craft: "They were excellent."

The shipping traffic got so congested the need to conduct repairs and marine–building services on a grander scale was becoming a necessity. The Town of Collingwood gave J. D. Silcox and S.D. Andrews $25,000 to open the Queen's Dry Dock, so named because it opened on the Queen's birthday, May 24th, 1883. It was a whopping 325 feet in length. The Queen's Dry Dock underwent many name changes, and changes in ownership. It will always be remembered simply as The Collingwood Shipyard. With the construction of large, wooden passenger ships, and later steel, W. Watts & Sons had a new and important client. Watts supplied a great number of the life boats used aboard these freighters and passenger vessels. With the connection by ship and rail, and now

the construction of some of the Lake's finest ships, Collingwood was truly becoming "Chicago of the North". Many towns claimed the mantle, but no other could compare to the level of activity at Collingwood. Watts' journey on foot to Georgian Bay was well worth the effort. The boats he created served a multitude of purposes. They

Collingwood fishermen prepare to leave for the fishing grounds, may 24th in the late 1880's. Sidewheeler Algoma *is visible in the background.* Collingwood Museum Collection.

were an essential part of the marine heritage of Collingwood, in fact, they were the earliest.

3. Joyce, Lorne. *Fish Boats Under Sail,* Island Seas–Spring 1997.

Natives using a Collingwod Skiff. Byng Inlet, c. 1908.
Huronia Museum, J.W. Bald Collection

5 WORKING BOATS

THEIR DESIGN AND FUNCTION

One of the most interesting aspects of boats, when mentioned in the same sentence with the Great Lakes, is the work boat. The work boat is arguably the first vessel to ply any Canadian waters by non-native peoples. Work boats have a colourful and diverse history. The variations of style and design are too large to define, at least in one book.

W. Watts & Sons seemed to be able to turn their hand to any style or variation in work boat design and construction. In the early days, the work boat was the Watts' yard stock in trade. William Watts' most famous design was, and is, the mackinaw, Collingwood skiff or Collingwood fish boat.

The wonder is always new

that any sane man

can be a sailor.

Ralph Waldo Emerson,
1803–1882
English Traits

Collingwood Skiffs and other Fish Boats

Of all the types of boats produced in Canada, particularly on the Great Lakes, and in later years, British Columbia, Collingwood fish boats have garnered accolades by all who know them. Undoubtedly brothers Matthew and William Watts were the first to introduce this type of fish boat to the Lakes. They incorporated many of their long-standing techniques of design and construction from native Ireland. William Watts Jr. states:

"My father was the first to introduce the Mackinaw fish boat to Georgian Bay...and I think you are safe in saying that W. Watts & Sons were or are the father of the Georgian Bay Mac...if ever a boat was designed for a particular body of water, it was the Collingwood fish boat." [1]

The vast, uncharted Georgian Bay was a force to be revered by any sailor, and to this day has the respect of any prudent and knowledgeable person who choose to navigate its waters.

Classic Collingwood Skiffs at Work in Parry Sound Harbour.
Collection Parry Sound Public Library

1. Captain William Watts to James Barry, September 15, 1937.

"The Collingwood Skiffs were soon famous for their speed and weatherly qualities, which allowed them to outrun or deal with sudden violent squalls which afflict Georgian Bay, for their shoal draft which allowed them to beach or fish in shallow waters, and for their easy motion when the nets were being lifted and the boats turned stern into the waves. Paul James Barry, in the important article written about Collingwood Skiffs says, "It is related that they would go to schooners anchored off shore when weather prevented the use of life boats. One story tells how, when they were refused permission to pass through the locks, Collingwood men who had been fishing in Lake Superior shot the rapids with their boats and arrived in Lake Huron whole and healthy, though a bit battered."[2]

An extremely seaworthy vessel, the skiff gained the respect and patronage of the fishermen who relied on them for their lives and livelihood. The reputation and regard for the quality of the boat earned a name that honoured the community where it was designed and built, Collingwood. These boats represented the pinnacle of excellence all around the lakes. Captain William Watts of Vancouver wrote:

"I have seen these same boats at their best and worst, running under bare poles for hours at a time, and I have seen them iced to their masthead and the sails crackling like magnetic sparks. I have seen them anchored in exposed positions and two men using buckets all night to keep them afloat. I have been on the bottoms and sides of them when they would not roll over entirely because the sails and spars kept them from going over entirely, and lashing ourselves on in a south eastern ten miles to the west of Collingwood in November.

I have seen us go to schooners anchored off Laferty Shoal in a fishboat when we could do nothing with a life boat. I was a member of the Collingwood Life Saving Crew for 10 years, and I am going to say here and now, properly handled, there is no type of boat made in the same class..."[3]

The Skiff ranged in size from 18' to the 40' 6" behemoths that were used in limited numbers on the lakes. "There were some mackinaws around 35 to 40 feet, which we built for different ventures on the bay,"[4] confirms William Watts Jr. Their versatility draws comparisons to Henry Ford's Model T. The only limiting factors in the use of the Skiff was the owner's own imagination. The Skiffs even gained the acceptance of native peoples of the time, which was an extreme compliment given the rich tradition and histories of the native peoples' designs. William Watts, when recalling the fish boats' use on the early lakes, said "I have known several Indians to own and operate Collingwood fish boats, both in Georgian Bay and Lake Superior."[5]

The boats were built of white cedar planking on steamed oak ribs, materials supplied by the boundless forests surrounding the region. Being double-enders, the fishing model was slightly beamier in the bow and finer to the stern. The yachting version produced in later years had a hull design with the same shape fore and aft, certainly a tribute to the design knowledge and attention to detail of its builders. Commenting on the design of *Nahma*, a Collingwood Skiff used strictly for sailing, one of her crew members, Lorne Joyce, says "She looks the same coming and going."

The clinker-built boat was the preferred type of construction, although numbers of carvel-planked boats were built as well. The clinker-built planking was preferred as it was stronger and did not require re-caulking every year, as the carvel- type craft did.

In recalling the evolution of the fish boat at Collingwood, W. Watts Jr. noted that boats increased in size as fishermen ventured farther offshore to set their nets. In describing a boat built for Arthur Clark, he said the boat was "clinker–built, 22 feet long, 6–foot beam and about 30"

2. Gillesse, Philip, *The Collingwood Skiff,*
   The National Museum of Science and Technology.

3. Captain William Watts Jr. to James Barry, April 2, 1939.
4. Captain William Watts Jr. to James Barry, October 10, 1938.
5. Captain William Watts Jr. to James Barry, September, 1938.

deep midships, centreboard and 2 sprit sails. And those were the days when Georgian Bay was teeming with fish and therefore did not require to go far offshore to catch. I think Alex Clark was the first to increase the size in the open boat. These boats were straight stem and slightly raking stern post, planked with white pine 1/2" thick and oak frames about 3/4 by 1-1/2" spaced 8" center with little finer lines aft than forward, slightly flared forward, making them quite dry in a sea way."[6] The planking of Clark's boat with pine would have been an exception to the rule. Most were planked with cedar. "We always kept in mind the shape of a fish,"[7] Watts reported, when noting the broader girth forward.

The boats were very shoal draft, being very beamy, shaping up to a fairly hard turn in the bilge. This gave the Skiff her ability to draw a small amount of water. The movable iron centre-board weighed between 200 and 300 pounds in the 26 to 28-foot boat. They were usually rigged gaff or ketch style and carried about 550 square feet of canvas in her sails. Any number of rigging designs could be found about the lake. Two masted being the typical set up, a single main was not unusual. Early versions were unstayed.

The boats were also fitted (out) to be propelled by oars, usually two pair. The reason for this was to aid in manoeuvrability on shoals and in tight harbours. The men could also row during slack wind or when reduced speed was required setting nets or lines. Ballast could be comprised of pig iron, bags of gravel, shale or stone. Roughly one ton of ballast was carried by a 26 to 28-foot boat. As a typical day of fishing progressed, ballast was tossed or shifted as fish were taken on, in essence becoming the new ballast for the journey home. In the rapidly changing and treacherous weather of Georgian Bay, speed was just one of the Skiffs redeeming qualities.

"Under sail the fish boats were fast, except to windward, sea kindly open craft of shoal draft centreboard lines. They were fore and aft rigged, most sparred with two masts and a long hogged down bow sprit. A 26' to 28' hull would carry 500–550 square feet of sail.

Rigs evolved over time. Early years saw the rig of the day –lug sails or sprit sails - on a cat ketch or a schooner. The foremast tended to be in the eyes and the after mast abaft the centreboard box. Gaff rig, often loose–footed on the boom at first, became the final standard, with gibs on bowsprits that grew from 9' to 12' in length over the years. The bowsprit was often hogged down by a bob stay that low-

A Collingwood fish boat entering the harbour. The early wooden grain elevator is seen in the background. Collingwood Museum Collection

ered the jib centre of effort."[8]

Fishing was not the exclusive realm of the Skiff. The boats were used as a transport vessel for all manner of

6. William Watts Jr. to James Barry, September 15, 1937.
7. William Watts Jr. to James Barry, April 27, 1940.

8. Joyce, Lorne. *Inland Seas*,
   Quarterly Journal of the Great Lakes Historical Society, Spring 1997.

Although the Mackinaw or Collingwood Skiff was a common sight in Collingwood harbour, the square sterned Huron boat (centre) was also built in large numbers. Collingwood Museum Collection

cargo. The 40–footers sailed in the Tobermory area, making the run from the tip of the Bruce Peninsula to Manitoulin Island. They served as mail carriers as well as passenger and livestock ferries.

A good boat builder is always open to new ideas, improvements and change. A number of alterations were made to the Skiff in the 1870's, when a man named Carmichael arrived in Collingwood from the Atlantic Coast. He had the Watts shop build a 33 or 35–footer for him. William Watts Jr. recalls:

> "She was by far the largest Collingwood fish boat that had been turned out. He had the forward 10 feet or so decked, and installed a couple of bunks and a stove below. She was rigged as a gaff ketch, with long bow sprit and unstayed masts, had a deck along each side and a very heavy wooden centreboard in place of the iron ones, commonly used in the smaller boats. She proved successful. Other fishermen liked her looks and a number of similar boats were built, though none was ever much larger. The average length of a Collingwood Skiff remained about 30 feet. In time, boats even smaller than that came to be rigged and decked like the larger craft. Carmichael's ideas put the finishing touches on the Collingwood boats. From this time on, they remained about the same." [9]

The East Coast would be influenced by this design and its success. The Skiff was likely one of the most widely-used boats second only to the Atlantic Dory in number. In the early 1900's, engines were added, which created a new dimension to the Skiff.

As the fishing industry ebbed and flowed, and eventually reduced to a fraction of its original size, the Watts Skiff kicked up her heels and was just at home in yacht rigging, racing the lakes alongside the pleasure craft of the day.

Philip Gillesse, traditional boat builder and small–craft historian, in a paper for the National Museum of Science and Technology states:

> "While not the oldest type of fishing boat on the Great Lakes, the Collingwood Skiff was one of the finest and one of the most popular, especially on the Upper Lakes. While copied widely by several builders, one builder, William Watts of Collingwood seems to have been both the biggest and the best. Of the thousands built, only one survives, the *Nahma*." [10]

The Collingwood Skiffs were the largest fleet of craft on the Lakes during the period of construction and use.

> "This type of fish boat is found on Lake Ontario as well as Georgian Bay, Lake Superior, Lake Winnipeg and other waterways right up to the mouth of the Mackenzie River. And I left one in James Bay in 1887." [11]

The Collingwood Skiff was not perfect by any stretch of the imagination. It was an open boat, exposing those who sailed to the extremes of the elements. Given the craft's design and purpose, the skiff was equal to almost any task.

Design features and rigging innovations can be praised and expounded on for an eternity, but the real credit goes to the expert skills and abilities of the early fishermen and yachtsmen who operated these craft. With experience called upon by preceding generations, combined with the sailor's own ability, the Collingwood Skiff can be recorded as one of Canada's most successful working craft.

Huron boat

The Huron boat carved its own niche in the business of fishing on the Great Lakes. By the 1860's, William Watts had been building the Huron boat for some years. In fact, modifications were made to some of Watts' personal craft they used for yacht racing. Racing versions had a much

---

9. Captain William Watts Jr. to James Barry, October 10, 1938.

10. Gillesse, Philip. *The Collingwood Skiff,*
The National Museum of Science and Technology, Ottawa Canada

11. Captain William Watts Jr. to James Barry, September 1938.

Pequod just out of the W. Watts & Sons shop. Pequod went back into the shop in 1997 awaiting restoration. Watts Collection

finer hull, and a substantially different rig than the working version of the Huron boat.

The theory behind the development of the square stern is open for debate and conjecture. Most will agree the addition of the cabin on the Huron was for inclement weather and dry stowage.

Square stern or transom of the Huron design opened up the work or cargo area of the vessel. The rigging had the foremast as close to the stem as possible. The main mast, which was slightly shorter, was usually located to the rear of the cabin hatch. Positioning of the main mast slightly aft of amidships, combined with the space created by the wide transom and full shape of the bilge, essentially created the work area required by the proponents of this design. The addition of auxiliary power made the Huron boat a very versatile craft by any standards. The customer could custom–tailor their Huron in sizes from 28 to 45 feet, an average 30–footer weighing roughly 6 tons.

In the early days the construction method used was clinker. As the design evolved carvel–planked hulls became the norm. Fantail and wineglass transoms could be added. A variety of bow configurations were also produced, with the plumb bow being the most popular. The typical Huron boat of 28 to 32 feet would have an 8 to 9 foot beam, and was constructed of cedar planks on oak frames. Huron boats were very pleasing to the eye, and well mannered in a sea provided the person at the tiller did not push the vessel's limits to excess.

In an article on Huron and Haywood boats in *Yachting Magazine*, James Barry states:

"This is an open-keel boat, moderately sharp forward, with a round bilge, rather short run, no overhang to counter, and a deep, heavy, heart shaped, square stern, with the rudder hung outside. She has less sheer than a mackinaw boat, and more room for nets, fish, half barrels, etc. The foremast stands as far forward as possible and is usually longer than the mainmast. The length of boats of this type are usually from 30 to 40 feet, with a beam of about 8 or 9 feet period. A boat 32 feet long and 8 or 9 feet wide would have a tonnage of about 5 tons...The majority of Canadian Huron boats had a long bowsprit, curved downward at the outer end by the bob stay, which, with the jib stay, was usually the only standing rigging the craft boasted, even when they had topmasts." [12]

As with all boats, one has to consider the design function and rigging set-up prior to judging the virtues or short-comings of a particular craft.

In 1862, Matthew Watts, brother of William, left Collingwood to establish a boat building business in Goderich. Matthew built an assortment of vessels, many comparable to the Collingwood operation. In a letter to James Barry, Captain William Watts Jr. notes:

"...the sharpie bow and the clipper bow are an off shoot of the other. Either of them making a good sea boat in a head wind because of the fact you can flair the bow as much or little as you like making them drive. But the square stern has but one redeeming feature, the roomy cockpit. It's no doubt an offshoot of the old fashioned schooner stern. And in passing I don't think I mentioned the fact before, but a brother of my father was one of the very early boat builders around Goderich or Kincardine. He was Matthew Watts." [13]

Lake Huron was a very busy lake in the 1800's. Fishing and lumbering were stable industries. Vast numbers of boats of all descriptions were employed on the developing shores of the Lake.

Lumber was readily available for boat building purposes with a number of local species being used: pine, oak, elm and maple to name a few. The slight difference in geography seemed to dictate the varieties of lumber used in boat construction. The Watts shop in Collingwood very rarely

---

12. Barry, James. Yachting Magazine, April 1942.
13. Captain William Watts Jr. in a letter to James Barry, October 20, 1940.

The Watts built Butcher Boy *is pictured here in Harbour Springs, Michigan 1938.* Henry N. Barkhausen Collection

This 1890's view of Killarney is typical of many early fishing villages around Georgian Bay. Many variations of size and style can be seen. Photo: Wm. J. Topley. National Archives of Canada PA 8555

used pine for planking, while in the Lake Huron region, pine was a common planking material.

Henry N. Barkhausen ordered a 30-foot Huron boat sight unseen from Watts' Collingwood operation. The *Butcher Boy* was delivered 5 and a half weeks after the order was placed. The purchase price was $700 in 1938. "The price seemed very cheap at the time, I had expected to spend about $500 on a used one." [14] When commenting on the overall quality of the boat to James Barry, Barkhausen said:

> "To me, next to her traditional appearance and nostalgic appeal, her primary virtue is simplicity. Representing a small investment, she gives tremendous value yet does not bother my conscious if I can't use her for months on end, or for several years, as the case may now be. She is rough and rugged and can stand both abuse and neglect." [15]

The influence brought by Matthew to the Lake Huron area would have a lasting impact as the 1800's drew on. The Huron boat was gradually displaced, losing ground to the larger capacity lake schooners and was eventually replaced on the fishing scene by the growing fish tug industry. After several years in Goderich, Matthew gained a well-deserved boat building reputation on Lake Winnipeg.

Scows, Barges & Schooners

Two of the most unromantic names on the Lakes given to a type of work boat, vital in the opening and development of the Great Lakes area, were the scows and barges. Although there is a century between the typical scow built in the 1870's and the bulk freighter built in the 1970's, many similarities can be drawn between the two vessels. Both the scow and the bulk freighter of today are relatively flat sided, with a slightly

round bottom, with in most instances a wide plumb bow. The purpose was to move a quantity of goods. A well–designed early scow was still able to manoeuvre surprisingly well, despite its generally unstreamlined appearance. With their centre-boards lowered, a heavy cargo sitting low in the hold acted as ballast, giving the scow unexpected mobility.

Some scows were built to an immense size, and capable of carrying tremendous loads. Cargoes of stone, grain and lumber were common.

W. Watts & Sons built a number of scows in the early days around Collingwood. Little is known of the quantity and sizes built. It is safe to assume that being the only commercial builder in the area for a number of years, Watts built their share, relinquishing the building of scows almost totally to other builders like Alfred and Bobby Morrill, and the Queen's Dry Dock in 1883.

This ship model, now in the Collingwood Museum Collection, is a massive sailing vessel, reputed to have been built by the Watts. It's name has been long forgotten, but the model shows a magnificent steam–sail schooner that graced the Lakes. The model was a conversation piece at Charles Duval's barber shop in Collingwood. Duval was a prominent black businessman, and had a clientele of successful men. The smoke emerging from the stack is actually hair, swept from the floor of the barber shop. Every customer had there own shaving mug, Watts' were among them.

14. Henry N. Barkhausen, interview with T. Marsh May 17, 1994.

15. Barkhausen, Henry, in a conversation with James Barry, April 1942.

Barge, loaded with provisions on the Magnettewan River. Possibly members of the Blackstone Hunt Club looking on, circa 1895.

Schooner barge, Mary S. Gordon *built on site in Kincardine by William Watts Sr. circa 1882.* Bruce County Museum, Ron Beaupre Collection

The lowly barge could be a former proud sailing vessel, passing its last seasons carrying cargo and being towed to all its ports of call. There is no record of the company constructing any large vessels for the barge trade. W. Watts & Sons did build numbers of barges, some up to 50 feet. Recalling his family's traditions, Reg Watts reported:

"My grandfather could turn his hand to the construction of any vessel. I don't think they ever refused or turned down a contract."

A number of small barges were built mostly for local

trade. They would be towed much like a utility trailer is hauled behind a vehicle today. They almost never had the honour of a name. Some firms would have a number of small barges to provide a form of custom haulage, transporting materials and goods, or even the family cow, to a remote location. The barge was not a sleek craft, but had to be constructed for heavy and abusive work over extended periods.

Schooners are not a vessel readily identified with W. Watts & Sons. One of the most graceful and versatile boats manufactured by them was the working schooner. Quite possibly the only close rival to the shapely lines of the working schooner were the racing sail boats and motor yachts designed and built by the Watts firm.

By the 1860's, the needs for a growing population and the manufacturer's appetite for raw materials made the small schooner quite valuable in the service of small settlements along the lake. The vessels acted as transports moving every manner of goods back and forth, making their deliveries quite often to individual families. Most vessels serviced the same customers–both commercial and private–picking up one cargo, delivering it and returning with another cargo from a different port. To many small communities on the lakes, the arrival of these schooners was often like a trip to town. Their relative small size and shallow draft made them perfect for access to the many shallow harbours and docks around the lakes. The *Mary S. Gordon* was but one of these vessels.

She was built on the shores of Kincardine in 1882 by William Watts. This 56-foot schooner had a long and exciting life plying the shores of Lake Huron and Georgian Bay until 1917. A significant career considering the loads carried and the never–ending work schedule she was placed under.

The schooner was a work horse of the lakes. Countless numbers served their purpose exceptionally well. When the age of power gradually eliminated the duties of these fine and distinctive craft, the Great Lakes lost one of its most romantic legacies.

Life Boats, Ships Boats & Life Rafts

In sheer numbers, the life boat was one of the most frequently built on a regular basis. The life boat contracts were controlled by the government and were not handed out at random. W. Watts and Sons had developed a business relationship and reputation for the servicing and filling of Government boat–building contracts that would last many years. The Watts yard had a very strict system of quality control: William's all-seeing eyes. The number of life boats being built was so great that an entire building was used for dedicated storage for finished boats. If the boats were not purchased locally by the Collingwood Shipyards or an affiliate,

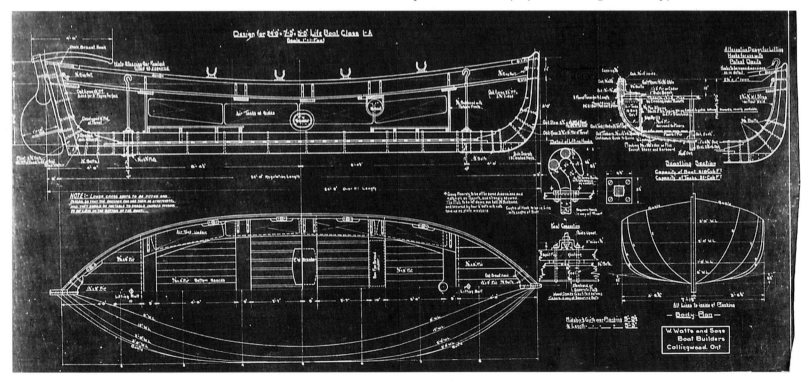

A 24' life boat, 1926. Note the breadbox and the number of air tanks.
Watts Collection

Corrugated metal life boats are hanging from the rafters and on the shop floor. The floatation tank is visible at the right.
The Barrie Gazette Magazine of Industry (1911) reported that Matthew Watts had over 2,500 sq. feet in the shop and that, 'specialty is made of manufacturing metallic life boats'. This newly constructed life boat is pictured inside the life boat storage house.
Watts Collection

Two fishing buddies out for an excursion on the Lake of the Bays. The man at the bow is Alexander Holmes, owner of this Watts row boat. Ken Holmes Collection

ESTABLISHED 1855

W. WATTS & SONS

BUILDERS OF

Wooden and Corrugated Metallic Life Boats

COLLINGWOOD,   ONTARIO.

We beg to notify the public that we have commenced the building of Corrugated Metallic Life Boats. Our boats are built according to the most modern design and in keeping with the Government's most stringent requirements and are of the highest standard in regard to material and construction. All boats are tested before leaving our shop.

Should you require any boats your order will be promptly filled and receive our most careful attention. An order is solicited.

W. WATTS & SONS

they were shipped anywhere on the lakes, including to U.S. clients. In fact more often than not, any photo of a lake freighter, passenger steamer or fish tug up to about 1945 would likely have been produced at the Watts yard.

Reg Watts recalls, "The boat house I am using was the storage house for life boats. This one was a storehouse, there was a cat–walk there from the main shop because it was all water here. There'd be eight or nine life boats stored here at once." The boats were hauled out with a block and tackle right out the door to the rail spur.

The boats were constructed under strict and specific regulations. Every part applied to the boat was stipulated on the tenders. From the type of hull paint down to the fastenings in the hull, nothing was overlooked.

In the early years the boats were clinker built, with about 75 % being double enders. The boats had a substantial amount of free board to help with the capacity they may have to carry in the event of a disaster. The boats could be rowed, the usual set up having 2 pairs of oarlocks with 4 oars. Both a rudder and a steering oarlock were part of the government's requirements. A mast could be stepped and a small gaff rig could be utilized if the situation required it. The rig was small to keep the boat from getting away from any person who might not have the ability to sail. They were equipped with grab ropes slung from the gunnels and handrails mounted on the turn of the bilge. The boats from W. Watts and Sons were usually shipped complete, unless otherwise requested.

A rare view of life boats being loaded from W. Watts & Sons life boat building, with the Collingwood Shipyard in the background. Another boat heads out of Collingwood for duty on the Lakes. Watts Collection

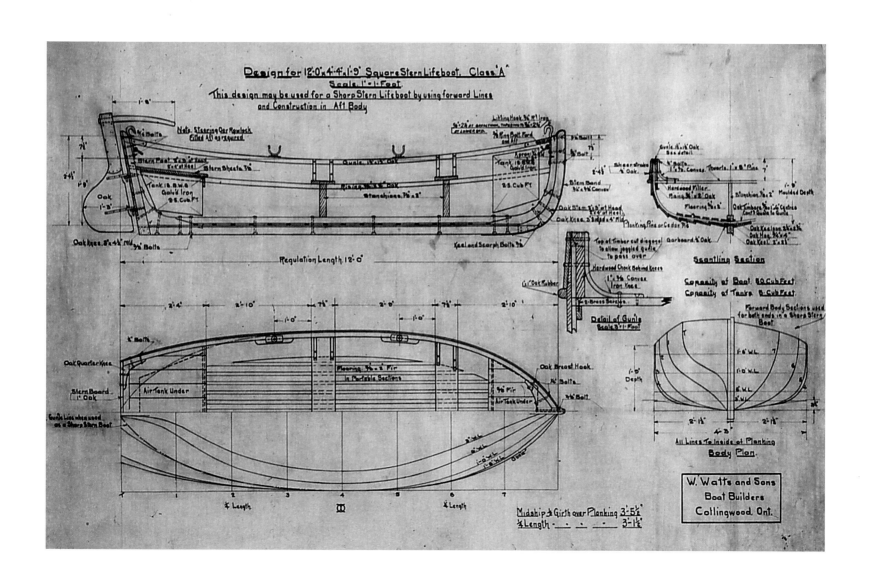

Plans for a 12' square stern life boat. Watts Collection

Fish boats hauled out for the winter, behind the Watts Shop. These boats are carvel, a more common constuction method in the 1930's. Watts Collection

Watts built fish boat with a cabin. There's still room aft for maneouvering outside the cabin. Watts Collection

The life boat business was brisk for the Watts boys in those years. The shop was building to capacity, often causing the work to spill out into the yard itself. One of the first major changes in life boats was the addition of copper and tin flotation tanks. The tanks were custom fit for each hull size and configuration. This task was up to the shop's tinsmiths to complete, who were kept very busy. Tanks even found their way into a number of

W. Watts & Sons shipped row boats to may locations for a multitude of uses. The sleek clinker built craft pictured here were used by Toronto Lifesaving Service. Toronto Harbour Commission Archives. PC1/1/10615.

Blankets, lanterns and even a built-in bread box appeared on some models.

Life boats ranged in size from 14 to 28– foot models with a huge carrying capacity. These boats were truly a massive craft. Chuck Parr, commercial fisherman, recalls, "I went to the Watts shop with Dad around 1920, I used to watch them put the ribs in, they built the life boats for the big ships on the lakes."

During the fast–paced development of the entire Great Lakes area between 1855 and 1895, lax government regulations, combined with the canal-style ships, made for a disastrous mixture. The *Asia* disaster in 1882 was fairly typical of the situation that was present in those days. Typical in that it was another wreck on the lakes that could have been avoided. *Asia* was not typical, however, in the number of lives that were lost. Most reports record a loss of over 120 souls. The *Asia* disaster was pivotal in launching shipping reform on the lakes.

Out for a days rowing around Collingwood harbour, prior to 1870. Collingwood Museum Collection

A variety of row boats used at Kew Beach. The Leuty Avenue Life Saving Station is under construction in the background.
July 19, 1920.
Toronto Harbour Commission Archives PC1/1/10644.

A Lifeguard oversees the women's swim meet in a Watts built life boat in Toronto Harbour, September 1938. The automotive building is visible in the background. Toronto Harbour Commission Archives PC1/1/5342.

Right:
Canoes and rowboats at the 30,000 islands near Midland.
Watts Collection

Dorothy Parr rows a Watts boat to collect the mail.
Chuck and Dorothy Parr Collection.

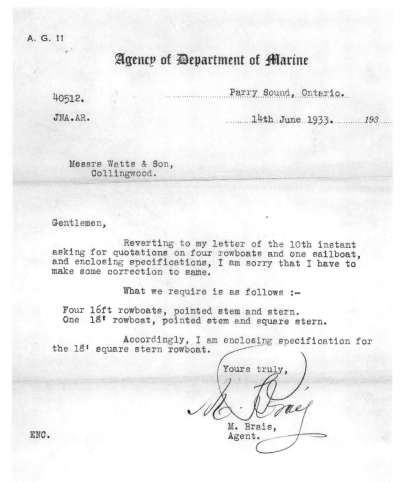

Agency of Department of Marine

40512.

Parry Sound, Ontario.

JNA.AR.

14th June 1933. 193

Messrs Watts & Son,
Collingwood.

Gentlemen,

Reverting to my letter of the 10th instant asking for quotations on four rowboats and one sailboat, and enclosing specifications, I am sorry that I have to make some correction to same.

What we require is as follows :—

Four 16ft rowboats, pointed stem and stern.
One 18' rowboat, pointed stem and square stern.

Accordingly, I am enclosing specification for the 18' square stern rowboat.

Yours truly,

M. Brais,
Agent.

ENC.

M. Brais of the Department of Marine requested 5 boats to be used as aids to navigation. Watts Collection

the Skiffs that were being manufactured, this of course at the request of the buyer.

The metal-smithing trade at the Watts shop would continue to expand, with the implementation of metallic life boats, the next major change in life boat construction. This was not only a boom time for filling new orders, but the life boats on the lakers years earlier were being replaced as well.

Many of the retired life boats finished their lives in a variety of interesting and ingenious ways. Some were equipped for commercial fishing, others were fitted with steam and gas engines, sails mounted and cabins added. A number of youth programs, one being Sea Scouts, used the life boats for sail training vessels. Retired commercial fisherman Chuck Parr says, "The life boat on our father's fish tug

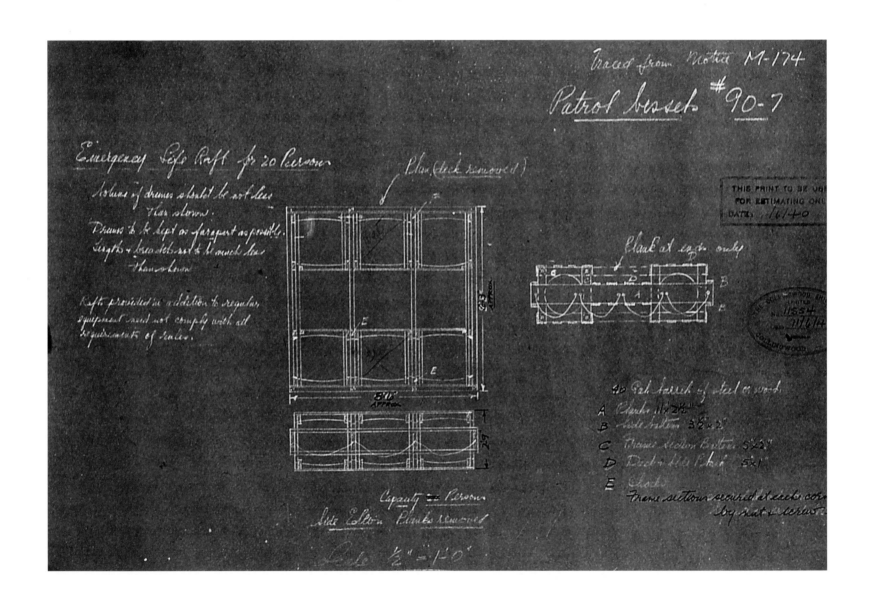

Many life rafts were built by Watts & Sons. These specifications were for the Collingwood Shipyard, c. 1914. Watts Collection

Dolphin, was a square-stern Watts life boat". The Great Lakes and Georgian Bay in particular, would see some of its first life boats built by Wm. Watts. This trend would continue from the 1850's through to the First World War and the Depression.

Brain and Art Drever, well–known commercial fishermen, recalled "Our tug the *Leighton McCarthy*, she had a Watts life boat on her, all the tugs up here had Watts life boats on them in those days. All the boats around the Bustard Islands fish ground were built by Watts." [16]

The larger passenger and cargo ships would often carry a combination of ship's boats and life boats, stored on davits or strapped in cradles. The ship's boats were usually square sterned, clinker-built like the life boats. Generally, they had a maximum length of about 22 feet. Ship boats resembled the classic Watts rowing skiffs, but were constructed with slightly heavier planks and heavier oak ribs. The ship's boats provided the larger ships a method of carry crew ashore, pulling lines to a mooring spot or just facilitating the movements of stores and supplies in an efficient manner. "They were just like seagulls in the lake the ones that Watts built. The doors were always open at the shop, and there was a lot of boats being built outside, most of them were double enders. Some of the boats had the 2 cylinder Dixon engines in them," said Parr.

Quite likely one of the oddest craft built by the Watts company in the lifesaving family of craft, were the life rafts. The rafts varied in size, with 12–foot square being the most common. The rafts were constructed to articulate and move with the waves under them and to conform to weight placed on them.

Row boats of Every Size

A tremendous number of row boats were produced by Watts during the century he was in business in Collingwood. About 90% of those produced were transom sterned, the elegant wine-glass shape an option. The clinker hulls were beautifully proportioned, with full keel and substantial skeg. The boats tracked beautifully on smooth water or rough, whether being rowed or under sail. The boats ranged in size from 12 feet to 18 feet in length. Some were constructed fuller amidships than others, always maintaining their beautiful sheer lines. Pat Johnston, retired Coast Guard employee, explains, "The boats had a lot of good freeboard at the stem and stern, she would float like a seagull. You very rarely got wet in them. The shape kept the waves out, even in a following sea, they could keep above it." [17]

Some of the boats were designed specifically for an engine, the shape being altered to allow for the weight of the engine and the full immersion of the propeller. Reg Watts recalled: "When I was a kid, that's all you would see in the harbour. The harbour was alive then, it isn't like that now. People just don't know what it was like, my family built a lot of row boats in those days ." [18]

Whether resting on a cradle, hanging from davits or bobbing behind on a tow line, these small craft have some of the best blood lines of anything afloat.

Lighthouse Tenders

As soon as the Department of Marine and Fisheries saw fit to light the lakes with a wave of lighthouse construction, the need to provide light keepers with water transportation also became necessary. Because of the absence of records from the boat building operation, it's difficult to determine exactly how many boats were supplied to the Department of Marine and Fisheries for this purpose. Many light keepers, however, know their boats were built by Watts of Collingwood.

Like so many of the other working boats, the lighthouse tenders varied in length and design. Jim Keith, light keeper for Nottawasaga Island, had a Watts 18–foot, clinker–built, double-ended boat. Keith recalls "There was a centreboard... one you could retrieve up and down and let your boat go level

16. Art and Brian Drever, interview with the authors, March 12, 1997.

17. Pat Johnston, in an interview with the authors, August 16, 1997.

18. Reg Watts, in an interview by Barbara Arp.

Department of Marine,

Ottawa, 22nd October, 1890.

CIRCULAR.

Sir,

With reference to the Boat which has been supplied you for the purposes of the Light, I have to inform you that the Department will hold you responsible for keeping it in good order, and painting it properly whenever necessary.

The Paint and other materials required will be supplied by the Department, and you are to include these articles in your requisition for Annual Supplies, but the painting must be done as part of your duty as Light Keeper.

WM. SMITH,
Deputy Minister of Marine.

National Archives of Canada RG42, Vol. 1532, File 7952-9

Nottawasaga light keeper Jim Keith is pictured here in the 16 ft. Watts built craft used at the light. He used it for two years before a motor was supplied.
James Keith Collection.

because we were in shoal area. There was a spar in it, about two-thirds of the way up forward, with a removable rudder. Well designed.....Boy, I tell you, let her go! You could take your children in it, you'd get splashed, but...." [19]

Light keeping had to be a family affair. It was isolating, endless work. The tenders were the only way onto the island at the start of navigation, and the only way off about a week and a half before Christmas. Keith and every other light keeper knew the wrath of the Bay, and had full respect when the winds started to blow. When the boats were on the lake and the wind started to pick up, they were hard to control because there was virtually no keel to speak of. Some refer to them as being almost flat bottomed, but they were not. The centreboard acted as a retractable keel. Jim Keith added there was "no skeg in them, and you get a little wind and there you are fighting to keep control...the more weight you had in her the more stable. Something I always carried was a sea anchor made out of canvas...it's one of the better safety features you can carry. You can be in deep water too and you can't get anchorage. The sea anchor, she checked you from rising too much and doesn't let you go cross ways. You don't hear too much talk about them any more." [20]

Coming off the light in December called for extra equipment. A pipe and an axe were good ideas to break the ice as they headed for shore. To ask a man and his family to sail across the Bay in an open 18–foot clinker built boat at the end of navigation was entirely unreasonable on the part of the Department. Requests from keepers to have engines added to their boats were denied. They literally risked life and limb to get home again. Most keepers applied a portion of their minuscule salaries for the purchase of a one or two cylinder engine. During the Second World War, the Department began supplying motors.

Western Island Lighthouse had its Watts tender built in the fall of 1907. The Western's tender was a 24-foot, double-masted, double-ended lapstrake boat. The 24-footer is clearly no different than the popular fish boats used throughout the previous decades, showing the versatility and stability of the design.

Later at the Western's, an 18-foot tender was used. Western's was solid rock. An ingenious A-frame winch was used to haul the boat up out of the water into a boathouse, where it was stored for the winter. When light keeper Jim Keith was asked how his children felt about spending their time on the island, he pointed to this picture and said "Do I have to say any-thing?" His daughter Susan, three when this was taken, does-n't seem to mind the isolation of the island. Behind her, a clear view of the A-frame winch is visible. The boat was hooked up front and back, picked up with pulleys, then the transmission was thrown in gear and cranked up

Susan Keith pictured here in front of the Western Islands boat lift. James Keith Collection.

by hand. "This had a triple rig block and cable. What it did, it would tighten up a cable from the back and would just draw up the boat like a string on a banjo. That would carry the boat up to the boathouse," [21] Keith explained. The 18-

19. Jim Keith, in an interview with the authors, January 25, 1997.
20. Ibid

21. Jim Keith, in an interview with the authors, January 25, 1997.

foot tender had a single–cylinder engine, or as some would note, a one-lunger. His boat at the Western's and the one at Nottawasaga were basically identical.

When asked what the original purchase price of the boats might be, Keith responded by noting "what they're worth for someone to buy them, who knows, but for some one who used it, their worth is far, far greater. Self assurance for your family, knowing that you could use it safely." [22]

Pat Johnston of Parry Sound recalls his father's work as the keeper at Caribou Island in Lake Superior. He described in a letter:

"The island is 130 miles north of Sault Ste. Marie and 64 miles west of the Canadian main land. From 1916 until 1921 he was obliged to leave the Island in December and return in April. This meant a 64–mile (trip) west across Lake Superior at that time of year. He was supplied with the sail boat in the photograph. To cross Lake Superior in this sail boat was out of the question, so he took out the masts and installed an engine, which he had to buy and pay for himself. He then added the cabin and raised the bow bulwarks. This was a Watts-built boat and withstood 5 return trips which I would say, speaks a great deal for the quality of the boat." [23]

Another tender, was entirely different again. The 18–foot, clinker built boat acquired by Larry Crawford for restoration has a wine-glass transom. Nine strakes per side

A–frame doing its work at the Westerns. James Keith Collection.

comprise her hull. This tender was constructed circa 1910 and is only in need of minor repairs. It was originally equipped with a motor, probably a two cylinder Dixon, manufactured in Collingwood.

In a report to the Minister of the Marine Department, the superintendent of lighthouses reported the number of "lightships" as they were called, their date of delivery and condition throughout the Dominion. The variety of boats supplied echoed the variety produced at the boat building shop. [24] The terminology varied from region to region. Some keepers reported they had "flat-bottomed boats", others referred to their boat as a "dory" and many reported having a "skiff". Most were delivered through-out the 1880's, and the craft referred to as skiffs varied from 15 to 28 feet long. At Goderich, light keeper Robert Campbell noted his 14-foot boat was new and in good condition, delivered in 1880. The boat at Pointe Clarke Station was a 22-foot sail boat with a 10-foot beam, also delivered in 1880. The keeper at Kincardine had a 17-foot boat, that was delivered in 1875 and now "very much out of repair". Jean Haitze reported that Lonely Island's 28-foot sail boat was in good order, delivered in 1882. Nottawasaga Island, just outside of Collingwood had two boats. One 14-foot skiff was not in good repair, and a 22-foot sail boat was also in need of attention after 6 years of service. Andrew Lockerbie's two boats at the Collingwood lighthouse were in good order, one 16-foot skiff and the other, an 18-foot boat. Luis Miron

22. Jim Keith, in an interview with the authors, January 25, 1997.
23. Letter from Pat Johnson to Tracy Marsh, October 10, 1995.

24. NAC, RG 422, Vol 1532, File 7952-9.

The Western Island light and tender. The glass plate negative used to reproduce this image shows with remarkable clarity, the consistency in the width of the planks along the boat's 24 ft. length. Photographed by M. Brais, Patrick Johnston Collection

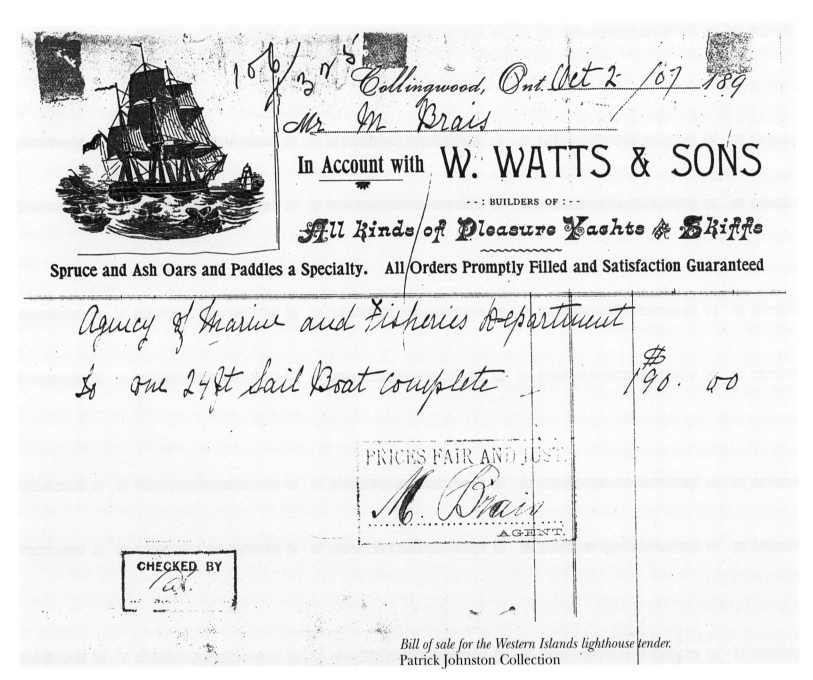

10 6/3 n s.   Collingwood, Ont. Oct 2 /07 189

Mr M Brais

In Account with **W. WATTS & SONS**

--: BUILDERS OF :--

All kinds of Pleasure Yachts & Skiffs

Spruce and Ash Oars and Paddles a Specialty.   All Orders Promptly Filled and Satisfaction Guaranteed

Agency of Marine and Fisheries Department

to one 24ft Sail Boat complete $190. 00

PRICES FAIR AND JUST

M. Brais

AGENT.

CHECKED BY

Bill of sale for the Western Islands lighthouse tender.
Patrick Johnston Collection

at Gargautua's Light was the only one to report he had a 22–foot 'Mackinaw', built in 1887.

When young Bud Akitt was looking for an apprenticeship opportunity, he turned to the Watts boat shop. He recalls a number of lighthouse tenders coming back to the shop for repair at the end of the season by Fred Watts. Cove Island, Hope Island and a few other boats were brought in. "The government sent them all in to get the planks replaced. We had to cut the planks out and replace them right along the water line. I guess we did four of them one winter – replaced the planks around the water line". [25]

One of the last boats built by Fred Watts was the 36 foot *Navaid* in 1943. Although it was built for Fred's personal use, he became ill and didn't have an opportunity to enjoy it. It was to take him to the Gulf of Mexico on a pleasure trip. Upon Fred's death, his son Reg purchased it for his own personal use from his Father's estate. She was carvel, transom stern and single masted. Upon launch, the motor was a 6 cylinder, Grey Marine Motor of 111 h.p. Reg used it until the summer of 1949, when it was sold for $3,970 to the Department of Transport for use at Prescott. It became the last lighthouse tender to be delivered by the Watts Boat Building company. It served as a light boat until it was sold by Crown Assets in March of 1968.

Specifications submitted to builders from the Coast Guard for tenders in 1944 called for a 24-foot boat, with a 7 foot 6 inch beam, 45 inches deep at the bow, 37 amidships and 44 at the stern. Carvel construction was the order of the day, with pointed stem and square stern. Keel was ordered to be of clear white oak or rock elm, 2 inches thick, 8 inches wide at the top, 4 inches wide by 2 inches below the rabbet, tapering and thickening towards the ends connecting to the stem, stern post and all the frames. Stern posts were to be clear white oak, as was the transom and the half-oval chaffing strip. Ribs were to be of rock elm or oak, 1-3/4 inch by 7/8 inch, spaced on 6 inch centres.

Four pages of specifications were delivered to the builders, detailing everything from fastenings to the waterproof cover.

Regardless of their size, propulsion or construction, the lighthouse tenders were a lifeline for the keepers, their families, and those in distress around the lights.

Ferries

Although not commonly seen around Collingwood shores, Watts Ferries were a welcome sight at remote locations in Northern Georgian Bay. The *Waukon* and *Ogana* were both constructed by Fred Watts. The first, *Waukon*, was a splendid steam-powered, double-decked boat. Fred Watts saw the expansion of the railway with the same spirit as his father William had over half a century earlier. When train arrivals were the only way cottagers could reach their weekend get–aways at Pointe au Baril, Watts took the *Waukon* and began a thriving delivery service. The name meant 'beast of burden' in a regional native tongue, appropriate for the ferry that carried countless heavy loads. Captain Watts delivered passengers and their freight from the train station to their cottages and hotels around the many intricate islands. *Waukon* began service with her creator and master at the helm in 1909. She was such a common site, and necessity for cottaging and vacationing in Pointe au Baril, often the boat is referred to as 'our beloved *Waukon*'. It was as much a part of Pointe au Baril as the cottagers themselves. Fred earned quite a reputation himself. Ruth McCuaig remembers Captain Watts well. She was a very young child when Watts delivered her Father from the rail station to their cottage. "*Waukon* was the first boat I knew," she said. "In the twenties it made two trips every day, it brought the mail every day... Eaton's delivered everything to your dock for free...from Toronto via the train and to your dock via the *Waukon*." [26] McCuaig's father was in business in Toronto. Like many of the businessmen who travelled north, he slept on the train since it was the last stop on the line. "On

25. T. Marsh interview with Bud Akitt, June 10, 1997

26. Ruth McCuaig, in a telephone interview with the author, May 30 1997.

POINTE AU BARIL TRANSFER BOAT

Express Rates

7 lbs. and under 20c
7 lbs. to 20 lbs. 25c
20 lbs. to 70 lbs. 30c
70 lbs. to 100 lbs. 40c
Over 100 lbs.
　　40c. per cwt.

Freight Rates

To Hotels and Main
Wharves---
　　20c. per cwt.
To Cottages---
　　25c. per cwt.

Steamer Waukon

Passenger Rates

To and from Hotels
and Main Wharves
including 150 lbs.
baggage $1.00
To and from Cot-
tages including
150 lbs baggage $1.25

Excess Baggage

25c. per 100 lbs.

Telegrams received from and delivered to the Post-office without charge. Telegrams will be delivered by us to your cottage if you notify us you want them delivered there at 50c. per call, if the cottage is on our route, and a higher charge according to distance if not on our route.

Pointe au Baril Islanders Association booklet featuring steamer Waukon.
Ruth McCuaig Collection.

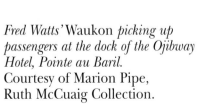

Fred Watts' Waukon *picking up passengers at the dock of the Ojibway Hotel, Pointe au Baril.*
Courtesy of Marion Pipe,
Ruth McCuaig Collection.

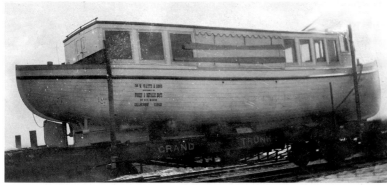

This sturdy passenger vessel is bound out of Collingwood. The shipping label on the boat says: ' for W. Watts & Sons, builders of Wooden & Metal Boats of all Kinds'. Watts Collection

Sundays some would take their fathers back to the station or be picked up by the *Waukon*...once the road went through, that was the end of that–which was a shame." [27] Even as a young child, Ruth McCuaig remembers Captain Watts was short tempered. With a busy delivery schedule, he did not tolerate anyone being late at the end of their dock. For many of the men, the time at Pointe au Baril was no vacation, there was always something to be done, mending screens, home repair, etc. In reference to her father, McCuaig said " by the time dinner came, and he got washed and shaved and dressed for the boat, he was always running late." [28] Her mother had a sure-fire method of diffusing Watts. Every Sunday night she'd prepare blueberry short-cake, made with fresh Pointe au Baril berries. It was seven year-old Ruth's job to take the offering down to Captain Watts at the end of the dock to buy her father some time, and placate Captain Watts. Naturally, a sweet seven- year-old girl delivering fresh dessert would not be turned away or discouraged. Ruth remembers "He wouldn't get upset having to wait, never mind the other passengers on board who were waiting." [29]

27. Ruth McCuaig, in a telephone interview with the author, May 30 1997.
28. Ibid.

This passener and mail ferry loaded on a grand trunk flat car for shipping is not under steam. A vessel in the shipyard slip behind this area creates the illusion. Watts Collection

Fred operated the Ferry *Waukon* until 1922, when he sold it to Jack Perks and Charles Griffey. The Reid family operated it for one more year, and the 'beloved' *Waukon* was retired in 1930. [30]

After his expeditions with *Waukon*, Fred Watts built *Ogana*, and operated it in very much the same trade. As was the nature with the ferry trade around Georgian Bay, boats and businesses were continually bought and sold.

Tugs, Mail and Survey Boats

William Watts Jr. made an overland journey through James and Hudson Bay in 1887. While there he built a 50-foot boat for the Hudson's Bay Company. In his letter to James Barry in November of 1937, he adds the following details:

> "The boat we built for our trip to James Bay was the only boat outside a small schooner used by the H. B. Co. for transporting goods from the parent ship that came out from London to the different smaller posts. She was about 50 feet. o.a., 16 ft. beam...the smaller craft were all birch bark canoes."

In 1842, a Geological Survey of Canada was initiated to conduct scientific investigations and field surveys. It was an endeavour that continued for decades. The purpose of the extensive survey was to determine the extent of Canada's natural resources. William Watts Jr. was contracted by "the

A. P. Low took this picture during the survey of Hudson Bay, 1899. National Archives of Canada PA146683

Geological Department to take a 30-foot mackinaw to James Bay in 1887." [31] Captain Watts not only delivered the boat, but was contracted to sail her during a summer for the Geological Survey conducted by A. P. Low. [32] The mackinaw was shipped to Missinabe Lake by rail. Captain Watts was assisted by fifteen natives to tow and row the boat to the head of the lake and down Moose River to Moose Factory.

"It took us two and a half months, but from then on I had a wonderful time, just sailing her where Mr. Low wanted to go." [33] On the return trip, the water levels had dropped so severely at Moose River, the party just beached the mackinaw and returned in a 30–foot bark canoe.

The Geological Survey being conducted in Lake

---

29. Ruth McCuaig, in a telephone interview with the author, May 30 1997.

30. Ruth McCuaig, *Our Pointe au Baril*, 1984.

31. Letter to James Barry from Capt. Watts, September 15, 1937

32. Vancouver Daily Province, April 19, 1952. *Stepping out at 90*

33. Ibid.

Also 4, 25 ft. whaleboats for survey.

R. WATTS
Collingwood

POST CARD

For INLAND POSTAGE only this Space
may be used for Communications

THE ADDRESS ONLY TO BE
WRITTEN HERE

Jul, 18th

C. ...ood.

Dear Uncle Will,

There are the
boats that Daddy
built for the Hudson
Bay survey.

They are 34 ft. long
8 ft. 6 in. beam. 6 ft
head room 34 h. p.
standard engine.
electric light. copper
fastened. finis...d
inside in butternut and
varnish

---

42 Maple St
R. WATTS
Collingwood

POST CARD

For INLAND POSTAGE only this Space
may be used for Communications

THE ADDRESS ONLY TO BE
WRITTEN HERE

The pole you see is
not wireless Tele-
graphy but just a
Telephone pole. the
man on the other
side is Uncle Mat.

I think the "Chemona"
would be swell to cruise
in. I wish we could.
what does "Chemona"
mean? Is mr. McKenzie
the bookkeeper. I'm sure
you will enjoy the trip
to Prince Rupert. Love to
all. your loving niece Emily

*Postcards to Capt. Wm. Watts Jr. in Vancouver from George
Watts' daughter Emily. In the top image, Matthew Watts can be
seen, standing to the right, making a final adjustment prior to
shipping. Collingwood Shipyard is in the background.*
Watts Collection.

Winnipeg during the 1890's by J.B. Tyrell was also familiar with the Watts name and product. Tyrell came to the defense of Matthew Watts after his sailing yacht *Keewatin* capsized while on patrols with the North-West Mounted Police. He was also one of the first to see Captain Watts after he was rescued from her overturned hull. One public attack was made against the seaworthiness of the boat, from a man who was removed from serving aboard her the year previous. Tyrell noted, "The charges made against the boat that it was unseaworthy are not true. The boat was the best sailing vessel of its size on the lake." [34] Tyrell had already brought two boats to Lake Winnipeg from Lake Huron. He declared if he ever wanted another one, he would "get Mr. Watts to build him such a vessel as the *Keewatin*." [35]

Survey boats for Hudson Bay were also shipped by rail from Collingwood. The image on the previous page illustrates the massive size and carvel construction of the boats. These survey boats were an indication of continued success with government contracts, a factor that would be a common thread throughout the 100-year operation of the firm.

As early as 1870, the founder of the company, William Watts, supplied a number of steam launches for the North West Territory mail route. It is unclear how many boats were supplied, but he was paid $2,036.90 for them, a regal sum of money for 1870.

During the last decades of operation, the company turned out a few more tugs than they had earlier. Early tugs can be seen along the water's edge near the Watts boat yard under construction, along with a variety of other craft. Fish Tugs were used prior to the turn of the century for fishing. Commercial fishermen switched to fish tugs for protection from the elements, to make room for bigger engines and predominately, to haul in a larger catch. For the children of commercial fishermen, fish tugs were a glori-

34. Manitoba Daily Free Press, Winnipeg. Oct. 17, 1890, *Matthew Watts is Dead.*
35. Ibid

DEPARTMENT OF THE NAVAL SERVICE
HYDROGRAPHIC SURVEY,
OTTAWA.

Ottawa, February 14th, 1912.

Gentlemen:-

In reply to yours of the 5th instant I beg to advise you that the launches we want built would require to be shipped from Collingwood by the 1st June to be in Halifax by the 20th June, as transportation is so uncertain.

As regards the cost you will remember they were equipped with a Standard motor engine and the Auditor-General's report states that you got $2475.00 for each. Before you submit any figure I would ask you to wait until I send you a blue print of the launch we require as there are some changes in it that may possibly change your figure although I think it should rather cheapen the boat.

You will probably also be required to figure on two gigs similar to those you had built for us before. I notice you received $235.00 for these at that time, but as they have been so satisfactory I would like to steer the order your way again.

Yours very truly,

Wm J. Stewart
Hydrographer.

W. Watts & Sons,
Collingwood, Ont.

This letter from the Naval Service illustrates Watts long standing relationship with Government departments. Despite the number of boat builders on the east coast, Watts still earns the comment, "I would like to steer the order your way again." Watts Collection

fied school bus. Art and Brian Drever recall heading to school from their family's fishing station in Britt. "There was no highway north of Parry Sound, so we had to travel either by rail or by tug. So they always came down here in September, and we'd always be late for school, or maybe some days we made it on time, but we travelled by fish tug, from Britt down here (to Collingwood) to start school." [36]

Fish tugs made good economic sense. Drever's tug carried 48,000 yards of net. "Before that they had unlimited yardage...they had what they called a tug license which was a gill net tug, which was like the old steam tugs in those days, and it was a 48,000 yard license." [37]

The fishermen of the depression era were equally as well served by Watts as they were in the 1860's and 70's.

The three fish tugs seen on the fringes of the Watts boat yard clearly show the evolution of the fisherman's craft. High cabins and transom sterns make room for larger catches, bigger equipment and motors.

The decline of the industry in general and the increasing spectrum of builders around the lakes, make it easy to see why fewer tugs were constructed than the double-ended fish boats of the last century.

36. Art and Brian Drever, in an interview with the authors, March 12, 1997.
37. Ibid

Charlie Parr on Umbrella Islands in 1927. "That Watts boat was like a seagull in the water," Parr said. Charles and Dorothy Parr Collection

Left: Fish Tugs hauled out for the winter, built by W. Watts & Sons. Gordon Clark Collection

Steamer Cumberland *sailed from Collingwood with an advance party of the newly formed North–West Mounted Police in early October, 1873. The wharf at Collingwood was the embarkation point for the new police force of the Dominion of Canada.*
Collingwood Museum Collection

6 KEEWATIN

THE MOUNTIES FIRST BOAT

Matthew, the brother of William and Jane, would be the first to leave the Collingwood operation. He initially set up a boat building shop in Goderich around 1862, making a name for himself on Lake Huron. From there, he proceeded to further his reputation beyond Ontario by heading for Lake Winnipeg.

"Ships are but boards,

sailors but men"

Wm. Shakespeare,
1564–1616
The Merchant of Venice

The Mounties, Watts and a New Marine Unit

Expansion west and the inclusion of Manitoba as a part of Canada amplified the need to enforce peace throughout the Dominion, as well as provide a civil force to help ease hardships weathered by new settlers. In August 1873, the North–West Mounted Police were established by an Order-in-Council with little fanfare. By the end of September, proposals were sought to determine how to move 150 men from Ontario to Fort Garry. Collingwood was chosen as the formation site for the first Mounties. It was a perfect location. Collingwood offered regular connections by steamship to Thunder Bay. From Thunder Bay, the recruits could head to Fort Garry.

On the docks of Collingwood the historic event went almost unnoticed. The first officers of the Police Force of the Dominion were issued their gear. Each was given one haversack, one knife, fork and spoon, one tin plate, a tin mug, one piece of soap and two blankets. They boarded the sidewheeler *Chicora* and headed north.

The newly-formed NWMP was established to forge a relationship with the Native peoples, keep the peace and contain the 'whiskey' traders.

Rum running was a growing problem on Lake Winnipeg. Illegal liquor was successfully making its way through Manitoba and north to the Territories. In the summer of 1890, the NWMP established posts in the District of Keewatin and elsewhere. Officers were given more supplies and equipment and eagerly awaited a shipment of canoes to patrol the waters of the district and curb the movement of liquor.

A simple canoe may have been effective for light patrols, but a commitment to regulating liquor movement on Lake Winnipeg required something more substantial. The NWMP identified the need to purchase a sailing boat for the task. In anticipation of this, a list of Mounties who had been sailors–or understood the management of boats–was to be delivered to Winnipeg. Only a handful of officers noted any marine experience on their enlistment information.

Matthew Watts was approached to solve the problem. Watts had built boats with his brother on Toronto Island, in Collingwood, Goderich, and now on Lake Winnipeg. It is unknown how many vessels he produced there. The sailing yacht *Keewatin*, built by Matthew Watts in 1888, was the perfect solution for the NWMP. A deal was struck and Watts' *Keewatin* was now considered a police boat. *Keewatin* was the first vessel to serve the force in this capacity and marked the beginning of the Mounties' new marine services.

As soon as the police contingent was established in the district, *Keewatin* and her skipper were summoned to Winnipeg. The vessel was to undergo revisions before her new duties on Lake Winnipeg began. Modifications were made, likely by Watts, under the careful supervision of the Inspector of the detachment, J.V. Begin. She was ready to start her career with the Mounties, as was Captain Watts, who would host the patrols with NWMP constables on board.

In a letter to Inspector Begin, Walter Robert Brown writes: *June 30, 1890*

"Sir,

I am instructed by his honour the Lieutenant–Governor to inform you that the Patrol boat *Keewatin* is now complete for service. The water ballast tanks and other fittings put in, it is his wish that the boat should proceed at once to the north end of the lake and commence her patrol duty. Mr. Matthew Watts, Boat builder esq., who has experience on the lake, has been engaged as sailing master, carpenter and guide, and from tomorrow, July 1, is wholly under orders."

Keewatin left for duty on the north end of Lake Winnipeg on July 2, 1890, with Watts at the helm. The crew on this initial tour consisted of Corporal Harry O. Morphy from Toronto and Constables Sabourin and Steele. Shortly after the journey began, *Keewatin* was in need of Watts' attention as a builder. Upon entering the shallow and rocky river at Selkirk, the centreboard was damaged. Captain Watts conducted the repairs over two days. The Inspector was satisfied with the work and returned to Winnipeg. Corporal Morphy received his instructions for patrolling on that particular section of the Lake and proceeded.

In 1890, lake travel was anything but predictable. Inspector Begin's return trip to Winnipeg was unexpectedly diverted to Grand Rapids. Along the route he met Constable George de Beaujeau, a new and young recruit from Montreal. George de Beaujeau and his party missed a train. With today's transportation networks, missing a train may be considered inconvenient. In 1890 the disruption was beyond inconvenient and translated into a potential two-week delay until the next boat would make the connection. For this reason, the Inspector jumped at the opportunity to travel on board a fish barge towed by a small tug and headed for Grand Rapids. The entire contingent boarded the barge and set out under the canopy of the Manitoba sky.

With little warning a disturbance developed. A strong head wind began and quickly escalated to a gale force. The captain of the vessel roared to the Inspector, "The barge is rolling so much I've twice seen the whole length of its keel, its broadside to the sea!" Then the captain panicked. He ordered the Mounties to drop anchor. The Inspector quickly hurried aft and forbade the men to even touch the anchor and tether their tiny vessel to the centre of the tempest. The captain recognized Begin's authority and wisdom. He conceded control of the vessel to the Mounties.

The new recruit, 18-year-old de Beaujeau and Begin took the helm and steered for five long hours. The barge made it safely to Grand Rapids with the crew and a shaken captain. This chance meeting and heroic display of seamanship gave de Beaujeau a unique opportunity to request a specific posting. He wanted to sail on Watts' *Keewatin*. Back home in Quebec, he sailed the St. Lawrence and told Begin he was quite accustomed to yachting. He made it clear that his first choice was to serve aboard *Keewatin*. The Inspector made no promises, but did say

he would advise him when the police boat returned to Grand Rapids.

When *Keewatin* did return, it was subject to another full inspection. Corporal Morphy and Captain Watts presented her ship shape. She was scrubbed, freshly painted and in perfect repair. Begin was so proud of the boat and the crew he proclaimed, "I take occasion to say that no better boatsman ever sailed Lake Winnipeg than Corporal Morphy!" Following the glowing inspection, Morphy requested the removal of Constable Steele from the crew. Morphy said Steele was unfit for any position aboard the boat and further that he "knew nothing about water."

The suggestion prompted Begin to recall young de Beaujeau and his request. Respectful of Morphy's skills as a sailor, and his leadership role aboard *Keewatin*, Begin noted de Beaujeau's request, but added that only Morphy could pick the men that would serve under him. Begin was heading back to York Factory and reminded the Corporal that as the ranking officer on board, he had to choose a crew that he found satisfactory. Coincidentally, Morphy also had a chance meeting with de Beaujeau in Regina when he joined the Force. The Corporal found no problem with him serving on board. The orders were prepared to switch Steele for de Beaujeau and continue the patrols at the end of Lake Keewatin until the end of August. Inspector Begin headed back to York Factory in a Peterborough canoe accompanied by one constable and two natives, hired as guides.

The crew of two Mounties and civilian Captain Watts continued their patrols. One brief stop on a reserve was apparently welcomed by the local Chief and Councillors. It was reported that simply the "presence of the red-coats had done a great deal of good."

By late July, a detailed schedule for *Keewatin* was forged. In a letter to Inspector Begin, Walter R. Brown writes:

"...His honour requests that you will, as far as possible, carry out the verbal instructions given to you, that you will take from Selkirk or purchase at Grand Rapids, a four-oared fishing skiff for the use of the party who will continue at that point. On your arrival there, it will be expedient to take such men as you select with the patrol boat *Keewatin* to Warrens landing and then place the boat in charge of your most competent non-commissioned officer with Watts as sailing master, and patrol the lake from that point to Poplar River, Long Point, Grand Rapids and such other rivers and places in the District of Keewatin as you may have reason to believe that illicit introduction of intoxicants have taken place. P.S. His honour desires that the patrol boat with policemen and Watts should reach the mouth of the Red River about the 10th of September."

All reports regarding the compatibility of the crew were favourable. Young de Beaujeau was pleased to be on the boat. Corporal Morphy was equally pleased with his performance. Captain Watts was more than a suitable companion and sailor for these expeditions on an unpredictable Lake. Watts' experience as a boat builder and navigator earned him the reputation of sailing master. The NWMP knew of his expertise owning and sailing schooners and smaller craft on the lakes in the Province of Ontario, and his cool and efficient manner when faced with danger.

In the early days of September, Watts' fortitude was put to the ultimate test. *Keewatin's* patrols were well documented by the crew and by those who had contact with them. It was an ominous sign when their whereabouts was unknown. The natives in the region notified the Inspector that *Keewatin* was reported to be wrecked. Inspector Begin left immediately to search the area for any survivors or bodies to be recovered. He met with Mr. Angus Mackay, an agent for the Indian Treaty No. 5. Mackay passed along the location of the wreck. Now Begin was faced with the grim task of surveying bits of wreckage washed along the shoreline. Articles which had been in the boat were pounding against the shore with every rush of the waves. He searched for any clues that would tell of the fate of the crew. There was no sign of them.

A search party was formed to intensify the efforts. Groups of Mounties were divided into teams. Some would continue a shoreline search, others would explore in canoes along reefs and islands. The Tyrell Geological Survey team which was working in the area at the time also joined the search. Tyrell, actually an old school mate of Harry Morphy, instituted a search between Pigeon Point and Catfish Creek. Inspector Begin's party reached Rabbit Point and encountered a man named Creight. He gave the first indication that any members of the ill-fated yacht had survived the ordeal. Creight reported that he

Crew and boat of Tyrell's Geological Survey, Pigeon Point, North side of Lake Winnipeg 1891. Geological Society of Canada. National Archives of Canada PA-038136

was given Matthew Watts by the natives that discovered the wreck of the *Keewatin*.

The unimaginable had taken place in the thirteen days that separated the disappearance of *Keewatin* and the discovery of Captain Watts. The fall of 1890 was a time of unusually heavy storms. Sunday, September 7th was one of those days that mariners talk about long after the journey is complete. The boat left Spider Island in the morning under heavy winds. By the time they reached Swampy Island in the afternoon it became clear that they should drop anchor. The storm grew and tore *Keewatin* away from the anchor chain and set the three men drifting over rough seas.

The seas rolled into *Keewatin* at a constant, pounding rate. Captain Watts stayed at the helm while Morphy and de Beaujeau bailed most of the night. The water came in as fast as they could bail it out. Their tireless efforts worked. *Keewatin* was still afloat by morning and so were the crew. Maybe all three were encouraged with the hope of a new day as the sun rose over Lake Winnipeg that morning. Perhaps the sun only illuminated the gravity of the situation to come. Winds whipped the Lake into a frenzy almost beyond imagination. *Keewatin* was driven hard into a reef and the centreboard snapped off. The merciless waters spun the vessel on end, leaving three men clinging to her overturned hull.

Watts, Morphy and de Beaujeau were exhausted, wet and without much hope. All they had now was each other and the hull of *Keewatin* . They cried to man and God to save them. George de Beaujeau, who desperately wanted

to sail on *Keewatin* , was overcome with fatigue. He slipped off the wooden hull and drowned. His career as a constable in the North-West Mounted Police was only four months, the last month on board *Keewatin*.

In this heavy situation, time must have stood still. No rescue boats. No search crews in sight. No voices crying their names from shore. Morphy and Watts spent their last evening together that Monday. By day-break Tuesday, Corporal Morphy, reported to be a 'gentleman' by his commanding officer, slipped into the waters of Lake Winnipeg. The physical and emotional suffering was too much. Knowing his time was at hand, Morphy reportedly looked at his friend and said "Matthew, I'm going. I hope you will survive to tell the tale. God Bless you."

Matthew Watts, the oldest of the three, now found himself alone. With countless sailing expeditions to his credit, and an intimate knowledge of his craft, Watts would have known the odds were against him. In an act that almost defies belief, the sixty-six year old Captain used supplies and gear that drifted with *Keewatin*, the line that had been left by Morphy, and literally strapped himself to her overturned hull. One wonders if he saw the irony in the situation. The master sailor, expert builder and creator of *Keewatin*, now depending on his own work to keep him afloat. Every sailor depends on their boat to keep them safe on the seas, but not this way. Not upside down, in a storm with nothing but a will to live.

Watts' ploy worked. For a time anyway. A full thirteen days after *Keewatin* broke loose from her anchor chains at Swampy Island, Watts remained lashed to the hull. He was without food, water or human companionship. He lapsed into unconsciousness. A local group of natives first spotted him on September 20th. They were sure he was dead. As they drew closer to the wreck and noticed he was still alive, they acted quickly and took him back to Rabbit Point. It was here that Creight watched over him for a couple of days until the steamer *Aurora* could transport him to the hospital at Winnipeg.

In the hospital, Watts made some progress toward recovery. Back on the Lakes, the search was still on for the bodies of Morphy and de Beaujeau. The Lieutenant-Governor offered a reward for their return, to allow for a dignified burial. They were the 15th and 16th Mounted Policemen to be lost in the line of duty in the 17- year history of the Force.

The ordeal was greater than Watts' tenacity. He became delirious and re-lived the events over and over again. As unbearable as the experience would have been once, Watts found himself perpetually reaching for his ship mates, begging them to hang on, trying to save them, crying for mercy. His tortured mental state lasted longer than his courageous battle with the sea. For Captain Watts, there would be no greater shame than the loss of his crew. He was tormented by his memory and the experiences aboard *Keewatin* for almost a month.

The search for the Mounties was fruitless. Young de Beaujeau's body eventually washed up on the shore of Lake Winnipeg two months later. The Lake never surrendered the body of Corporal Morphy.

Captain Watts' endless cries for mercy were granted.

He died October 15 in the hospital at Winnipeg. Inspector Begin had this to say about Matthew Watts:

"The sailing master of the patrol boat, Captain Watts, aged sixty-six, after remaining tied to the wreck for days, was rescued alive and conveyed to Winnipeg hospital, where I saw him, and heard from his own lips the tale of the wreck and his subsequent sufferings. His ability as a sailing master was undoubted, and his efforts to sustain our men after the accident cannot be too highly extolled, while his fortitude during the awful time he remained tied to the wreck almost surpasses belief. I regret to report that after rallying, and apparently rapidly approaching recovery, this fine old man had a relapse, and succumbed to the results of the frightful exposure and sufferings which he had undergone."

The skills and abilities of the sailing master were never called into question. Begin filed this report:

"I was well acquainted with the patrol boat *Keewatin* having sailed with her last year on her first trip to Grand Rapids; and although we encountered much stormy weather, I never saw a boat that behaved better in a heavy sea and with a high wind. I have since sailed in her and my former good opinion has been increased and I do not think that any boat could have been better sparred or fitted with a better rig or better proportioned canvas, or as well found in all necessary ropes, anchors and chains. I have lately seen her on the bank at Selkirk, and after a careful examination I found that with the exception of where the rocks

File   7070.

Custom House, Winnipeg.
29th October, 1890.

Sir,

I beg leave to herewith forward you the official report of casualty to yacht "Keewatin" which occurred on Lake Winnipeg about the 16th of September.

This report is made by His Honour, Lieut-Governor Schultz, all the officers that were on the vessel being dead.

No value is placed on the damage to the vessel itself, but as the loss was only the centre board, bowsprit, &c. I would say that fifty dollars would cover damage to vessel

I have the honor to be
Sir
your obedient servant
Thos Scott
Registrar

To the Deputy Minister
of Marine
Ottawa.

National Archives of Canada RG18
Portion of Vol. 1194
File RCMP 1890
numbers 423–432

The General Hospital in Winnipeg, where Captain Matthew Watts was taken after the wreck of the Keewatin. Photo by Albertype Co. National Archives of Canada PA-031530

rubbed against her on the port side near the waterboard, she is almost wholly uninjured, except, of course, the centre board, which was broken off when the boat struck the reef upon which she was wrecked."

Keewatin had travelled over 1,000 miles that summer. Tyrell, the leader of the Geological Survey team that was in the area at the time, also proclaimed the virtues of the boat. He noted there was no finer boat on the Lake, and if he were going to have a yacht built, he would have had Matthew Watts build him one just like *Keewatin.*

The Inspector noted that in the District of Keewatin in the summer of 1890, due to the patrols and presence of the NWMP, no liquor had passed without a proper permit, and no crime had been committed.

It wasn't a crime to have uncharted waters in 1890, in fact, it was commonplace. The fate of the *Keewatin* and her crew may have been averted if a chart of the Lake was available. The only aid to navigation on Lake Winnipeg was a single lighthouse, between Red River and York Factory. One tiny beacon, a huge expansive lake almost as big as Lake Erie. One light for the third largest lake situated entirely within Canada. Lake Winnipeg occupies over 24,000 square km (9,417 sq. miles) and is over 400 km (264 miles) in length. Sailors had no indication where shoals, sandbars and reefs were located. Navigation was treacherous by day. At night, it was pure madness. *Keewatin* was not the first disaster, nor would it be the last. A steam barge, *Red River*, ran aground on a sandbar during the summer of 1890. The passengers and crew waited three weeks before a rescue crew reached them.

To replace *Keewatin*, Inspector Begin suggested that a steam craft be constructed. He felt this kind of boat would provide the flexibility and speed needed for the "evils" of their work. The steam craft, according to Begin, would be more efficient for rescuing and have increased manoeuvrability on the uncharted Lake.

POSITIVELY
NO SMOKING
ALLOWED.

CHICORA
OF
COLLINGWOOD.

Collingwood's Chicora *at home port.* Chicora *was used
by Col. Wolseley as a troop transport for the Rebellion.
Notice the activity under the 'No Smoking' sign.*
Collingwood Museum Collection

7 THE 1870 REBELLION

BOATS FOR THE RED RIVER ROUTE

Upper Canadians' love affair with the railway was flourishing by the 1860's. The huge locomotives made a grand entrance each time they rolled into rail stations throughout the Canadas.

"Look also at ships: although they are so large and are driven by fierce winds, they are turned by a very small rudder whenever the pilot desires."

James 3:4

Dominion from Sea to Sea

In the fall of 1864, the idea of a Confederation was discussed at Charlottetown. On July 1, 1867 the Dominion of Canada was born. The new Premier of New Brunswick marked the occasion quoting the Bible "He shall have dominion from sea to sea and from the river to the ends of the earth." If this was to be so, there was still a huge mass of land between the seat of government in Ottawa and the Pacific Ocean. The movement to acquire western territories as part of the Dominion began.

Manitoba became part of the Confederation by spring of 1870. The rail lines allowed people to move west with relative ease. For some, the expansive, unpopulated regions of Manitoba held a chance to establish farms, businesses and homesteads as pioneers, like some of the settlers in Canada West, had done decades earlier.

The Métis in Rupert's Land, the new Manitoba, had no intention of giving up their land so freely to surveyors from Ottawa. Led by Louis Riel, the Red River council was formed and began to negotiate with Ottawa. Riel was a young, fiery leader who took up the mantle to fight for the rights of the Métis for their land, culture and religion. The Canadian Government failed to notify the settlers of Red River that their lands were now transferred to the federation from the Hudson's Bay Company. The Métis were known as 'half-breeds', French–speaking, Catholic settlers. Riel was challenged by another group at Red River, the English

Protestants from Ontario. Defiance of Riel's authority lead to the execution of Thomas Scott, an outspoken Englishman from Ontario. *The Canadian Illustrated News* ran engravings showing Scott being blindfolded, laying face down on the ground and shot at nearly point blank range. English–speaking Canada was outraged.

John A. Macdonald, the first Prime Minister of the new confederation, was already considering sending a military force to Red River to aid in the expansion of the country. Now, with the public outrage at the shooting of Scott, Macdonald had no choice. Rumours abounded that Scott died a slow, painful death. Riel was seen as a cold-blooded killer who had to be stopped. Every newspaper in the land covered the events. The *Collingwood Bulletin* published first-hand accounts of Mr. Farquahar McLean, originally of Portage La Prairie. He had made the trek to Lake Huron to purchase a grain separator in the town of Clinton, to take back to his Red River Farm. Regarding Scott's execution, the *Bulletin* reported:

> "McLean was a prisoner at Fort Garry when poor Scott was shot, and although naturally reticent about politics, he says the rumours about Scott lingering so long after he was shot are pure exaggerations. He (McLean) was one of the party that left the Portage to release the prisoners at the Fort, and was captured by Riel's half-breeds and imprisoned in the Fort." *July 20, 1870.*

Rumours also abounded that the fertility of Rupert's Lands were unfit for farming. McLean said "This is an abominable lie". He went on to report that he had farmed 500 acres for a decade and yields 40 to 60 bushels of prime wheat per acre, in sharp contrast to the maximum of 24 bushels per acre that was being depicted in the press. McLean felt that due to the quality and depth of soil and expanse of the land, the soils were "practicably inexhaustible."

The acquisition of these lands, and more critically, the quelling of Louis Riel led to the mobilization of the newly-formed Canadian militia. The ink was barely dry on the legislation when volunteers were called into action.

S. J. Dawson, Civil Engineer, was in charge of the transportation for the expedition, under the command of Colonel Garnet J. Wolseley, a popular British staff officer. Two battalions of militia, engineers, guides and teamsters were assembled. In the spring of 1870, Parliament was assured that this expedition was not intended to result in battle. The goals were to assure the people of Red River, and the numerous Indian tribes, that they were welcome in the new British Dominion. The Metis saw the advancing of the militia as punitive, and Riel fled.

The movement of troops would have been easiest through the canal at Sault Ste. Marie. Americans, sympathetic to Riel's cause, denied the militia the use of the canal for transport of any war supplies or troops. This left Dawson with only two options for a route to the Red River, both of them were long and treacherous. Two hundred miles of the route chosen had never been navigated by anything larger than a bark canoe. The Dawson Route, as it became known, called for navigation across Lake Superior and up to Red River. Collingwood became a major launching point for the expedition.

The busy port town was an obvious choice, with major connections by lake and rail. Many supplies were shipped by rail from Toronto to Collingwood and then by steamer north. The *Algoma* and *Chicora* were both used to transport troops and supplies during the 1870 expedition. Other supplies, including carts and cattle feed, were purchased from suppliers in Collingwood. Goods were purchased through the Department of Public Works, or through a special account of the Manitoba Expedition under the auspices of the Militia.

The complexity of the Dawson route, the long portages, rapids and steep inclines meant that a number of small boats had to be used to transport troops and supplies. Dawson requisitioned the support of "principle" boat builders from Ontario and Quebec for the task. The specifications and contracts were given out in January and boats were to be delivered by the opening of navigation.

In Collingwood, William Watts was given a contract for 9 boats. R. Benoit, who built boats in Collingwood for a short period

of time, was contracted to build 6. Only Samuel Leves of Toronto built more boats for the expedition than Watts, who delivered 15 in total. Boat builders from Barrie, Hamilton, St. Catharines, Port Dalhousie, Welland, Owen Sound and Kingston also participated. The boats were 30 feet in length, 6 1/2 feet on the beam with a depth of 32 inches. Each was capable of carrying 2 1/2 tons when loaded, twelve men and all their gear. A total of 135 boats were used for the expedition. Dawson noted that the actual tonnage of the 30–foot keel boats, by shipbuilder's measurement, would be 5 tons.

Route of the Red River Expedition: McKay's Mountain, Thunder Bay, Ontario. Note craft in tow, built specifically for this expedition. Royal Ontario Museum

In Wolseley's "Story of a Soldier's Life" he illustrated the need for strong boats because of the treachery of the route:

"The total distance to be traversed between Port Arthur and Fort Garry was over 600 miles, and the range of hills that we had to cross, and which divided the waters which drained into Hudson Bay from those that reached the sea by the St. Lawrence river, was about 800 feet in height. Everything depended upon how the force to be employed was organized and equipped before starting. After we had once embarked in our boats on Shebandowan Lake, we should be cut off absolutely from all outside help and should have trust entirely to our own exertions and luck. On the way to Fort Garry we could not receive reinforcements, and, worse still, could obtain no provisions, clothing, ammunition, axes or other tools. Everything we required had therefore to be taken with us in our boats and their carrying capacity was necessarily very limited. All implements for use during the expedition had to be both strong and light. At the numerous rocky and difficult portages to be traversed, our boats would be exposed to extremely rough usage, for which they would have to be well built of good tough material."

Wolseley rightly noted if the boats were constructed heavy for the purpose of carrying additional supplies, they would have been too heavy to portage over steep and rugged heights between Lake Superior and Winnipeg.

There was virtually an equal split between carvel and clinker-built boats. The method of construction of these boats was also the subject for great debate. Which boat would be stronger, carvel or clinker? Of the boats that were shipped from Toronto to Collingwood by rail, many sustained damage just from the rail cars. The Toronto *Globe* joined the debate by noting "the opinion of some who have already travelled the route is that the clinker-built boats will be useless." [1]   There is no documentation to suggest that Watts built his 9 boats one way or another. With his experience and expertise in the use of a clinker boat, Watts likely extolled the virtues of clinker over carvel. When properly built, no caulking was required to seal the seams from one plank to another. They were also seen to withstand more abuse being pulled up on a rocky shoal. William Watts Jr., who reports he was too young to help build the boats in 1870, said he helped put nails in the holes so the men could drive them in. He was just 8 at the time. Pondering the clinker versus carvel argument, Watts said "The clinker is the stronger boat of the two and easily kept tight, but takes longer to build. They are also better sea boats, and livelier in a sea. The lap has lifting power. These boats are more difficult to build on a solid mold, hence the greater number of carvel are used." [2]   Whatever the case, there were equally good reasons to use both kinds of construction, and both were equally represented in the expedition.

Standing orders for the Red River Expeditionary Force

---

1. Toronto Globe, May 4, 1870
2. Captain William Watts Jr. to James Barry, November 1937.

Collingwood, 21 May 1870.

Dept. Public Works
per S. J. Dawson
in a/c with Geo. Smith

Scow a/c

R. Chapman 9 days @ $2		18.00
W. Watts 8 " " 1.75		14.00
Jas. McLaren 9 " " 1.50		13.50
F. Bassett 9 " " 1.50		13.50
Expenses to Stayner		1.—
Telegrams 1.— Mails 25		1.25
Loading Cars .75 unloading do 1.30		3.05
One Auger .50 Pitch Pot .80		1.30
R. Kennedy for pump		10.—
P. Lye for Blacksmithing		6.90
Wood for Rudder & Handspikes		1.—
Washers		.50
Hardware Thos. Long & Bro.		41.92
Superintendence — 13 @ $2		26.00
+ for Slats		.30
3 days at Penetanguishene		6.—
	$	158.77
Less by Cash		100.00
	$	58.77

Received payment
George Smith

Witness
A. L. Russell

Unloading stores at Prince Arthur Landing.
Royal Ontario Museum

*Account for building a Scow at
Sault Ste. Marie.
Lists W. Watts wages at $1.75 per
day for 8 days, and hardware
from Thos. Long, $14.77*
National Archives of Canada,
RG9 II, F3, Vol.3.

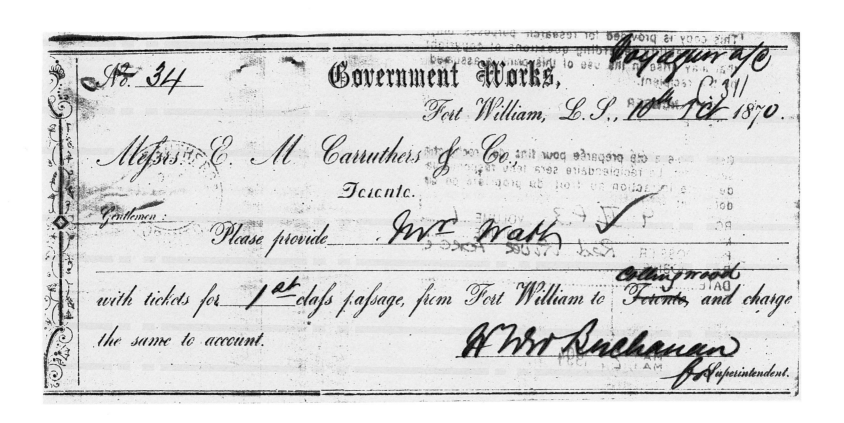

William Watts ticket home aboard Algoma, *1st class*
National Archives of Canada RG9 ll 83 Vol. 1 File: Red River Force.

list the following tools and equipment to be loaded aboard each boat: "2 felling axes, 1 pick axe, I spade, 1 shovel, 2 hand axes, 2 flanders kettles, 2 frying pans, 2 sails, 2 boat hooks, 2 spare oars, making eight in all, 4 row locks, 1 set of blocks (single and double), 1 boat lamp, 6 thimbles for setting poles, 1 dipper, 1 rubber bucket, 1 boat sponge, 2 cans paint (black and white), 5 lbs. assorted boat nails, 1 double tin oil can, 1 tin with pitch, 1 tarpaulin, fenders, 60 fathoms tow line, 1 can mosquito oil etc., spare plank and tools necessary for repairs. There will also be the cooking utensils of the boatmen, for which the coxswain of each boat will be responsible. In every boat there will be 30 days' rations for the soldiers and boatmen, besides also, about 1 ton of surplus store." [3]

Aside from the 30-foot keel boats used to transport men and their equipment, a series of flat scows were ordered for use in shallow rapids. One particular scow was built at Sault Ste. Marie in account with George Smith. William Watts participated in the construction of the scow on site at the Sault. He was the second highest paid boat builder on the payroll at $1.75 per day. Watts spent 8 days in the Sault for a total payment of $14 for the work done. Another Collingwood firm was involved in the scow construction. Thomas Long & Brothers supplied over $40 of hardware for the job.

The debate over the seaworthiness of the boats and the complexity of the route called for skilled voyageurs to manage and navigate the boats. The men engaged as voyageurs had significant experience navigating inland waters, driving logs and ideally, boat building skills. For all these reasons, William Watts was retained by the Dominion as a voyageur from June 30 to October 14th. He was paid $235 for his services over the three and a half months, and was sent home aboard the *Algoma*, first class. Most of the other voyageurs travelled home second class.

Voyageurs helped to guide the boats and supplies all the way to Fort Garry. The boat builders, however, were stationed at some of the more difficult portages in order to repair damaged boats and scows. Typically there were three voyageurs to a boat, one acted as coxswain.

Watts was away from Collingwood for almost a year serving in the 1870 rebellion. Family tradition notes that he was superintendent of "a number of boats" during this time. "His services upon the occasion were so highly satisfactory that they merited and received the personal approbation of the commanding officer." [4] In 1899, the Government authorized the issue of a service medal for those who served in the 1870 Rebellion. William Watts of Collingwood was the proud recipient of one of these Canadian general service medals.

3. Standing orders for the Red River Expeditionary Force Toronto, 14th May 1870.

4. *William Watts is Gone* Collingwood Enterprise.

Captain Patrick Doherty is coxswain of the Collingwood Life saving crew in this 1893 photo. George Watts is seated at the stern and Matthew Watts is in the aft seat manning an oar. There were up to 5 members of the Watts family serving at the life saving station at any one time. Collingwood Museum Collection

8 ARTHUR & THE ASIA

MARINE DISASTER HITS HOME

"Those who go down to the sea in Ships, who do business in great waters, They see the works of the Lord, and his wonders in the deep"

Psalm 107: 23-24

Local mariners, fishermen and boat builders were the only life-line for passengers and crew on an increasing number of marine disasters on the lakes. Men who intimately knew the uncertain waters were obvious candidates for rescue work. By 1882, the first Life Saving Station was established in Coburg. Collingwood's Life Saving Station was established in 1885, and at the time was the only one located on Georgian Bay. Prior to the stations, rescue efforts were organized within the community and were conducted primarily in wooden fishing boats.

William Watts frequently found himself on the front line of rescue efforts out of Collingwood.

In August 1863, long before the government introduced basic safeguards for lake navigation, the steamer *Ploughboy* failed to make the scheduled stop at Collingwood. Those who were waiting along the docks for *Ploughboy* to arrive became more troubled as time passed without sight of the ship. Watts was dispatched to find the vessel along with W. Miller, W. G. Paterson, John Albiston and David Miller. Winds made it impossible for their vessel to make any headway. The engineer of *Ploughboy* managed to travel from the vessel to Collingwood by canoe. He reported the steamer to be disabled and laying at anchor about fifty miles north of Little Current. Four people drowned.

On the evening of November 24th, 1872 the steamer *Mary Ward* ran aground on Mulligan's Reef, just west of Collingwood. She was making her way to Collingwood with the 27 passengers and crew when she hit bottom. One life boat was launched and safely reached the shore. Rescue operations to the site were delayed by a sudden gale. A second life boat landed safely after an unpleasant journey, and a third capsized, drowning all eight aboard.

Captain George Collins and Frank Moberly were finally able to launch their

A young and fiery Captain "Black Pete" Campbell. Black Pete, was a long time friend of the Watts family and they were neighbours on Maple St. in Collingwood Collingwood. Museum Collection

rescue party of 15 volunteers. Among the crew were eight members of the Masonic Lodge, including William Watts. They went to the scene in fish boats and rescued the nine who were left on board *Mary Ward*. Canadian Parliament rewarded the 15 men with commemorative medals and $15 each for their actions.

There are few lake disasters that rival the enduring allure of the loss of *Asia* in 1882. It was not the greatest loss of life on the lakes, but with over 120 lives lost, the toll was very high. It was the biggest disaster on Georgian Bay. It was a time when wrecks were increasing in frequency and number. In preparing to describe the event, the Collingwood *Enterprise—Messenger* reported:

> "It is difficult to speak or write of this soul-revolting tragedy without feeling a shudder at man's apparent helplessness to avert such disasters. Time and again we have had to record these frightful losses of human life, and the task becomes heavier and more sickening with each repetition."

Of all the wrecks and rescues Watts was called to, the *Asia* would leave the most indelible impression on his household.

The story of *Asia* is truly a Collingwood tale. She was purchased by the Great Northern Transit Company to replace *Manitoulin*. *Manitoulin* was under the expert care of Collingwood's own Captain Campbell, known as "Black Pete".

"Black Pete" earned his nickname with a thick, dark beard and captivating deep brown eyes. He was a fierce competitor and had a reputation for a similar temperament. His deep fog-horn voice struck fear in the heart of many young sailors. Under a gruff exterior was a kind, gentle man with a sentimental heart of gold.

A bustling Collingwood Harbour. Steamers Northern Belle, Atlantic *and* Wiarton Belle *form a back drop to the massive fishing fleet. Passenger traffic by the lake was nearing its peak.*
Collingwood Museum Collection

Asia *docked alongside* Ontario *c.1882.*
Collingwood Museum Collection

Great Northern Transit Company's Emerald, *one of the three steamers owned by the company.* Collingwood Museum Collection

Captain Campbell was as keen in business as he was on the lakes. He pursued his own navigation line after a term as Captain of the *Waubuno*. He saw an opportunity to form a new transportation company and run competition to the existing Beatty Line by adding another steamer from Collingwood to the Sault. The Georgian Bay Navigation Company was formed in Collingwood. Campbell's partners included Thomas Long, J. J. Long, and Charles Cameron. They purchased a ship state side and named her *Northern Belle*. All three men later became primary investors in the Collingwood Dry Dock and Wrecking Company, which evolved into the Collingwood Shipyards. Eventually, the competition line merged with the Georgian Bay Navigation Company and the new entity was known as The Great Northern Transit Company.

"Black Pete", not surprisingly, became commodore of the fleet. Captain Campbell's ships made it from one port to another in record time. His escapades as Captain of *Pacific* were reported frequently. In 1892, a Manitoulin Island paper, in reporting that *Pacific* had beat the *City of Midland* by 5 minutes and 37.12076 seconds from Owen Sound to Collingwood, stated:

> "You could see the Cap's smile half way to Strawberry shining like the church steeple and his chin whisker was sticking out at an angle of 90 degrees with excitement, while his hat was tied on with a stout piece of hawser, and in each boot was a flat iron to keep him from blowing off the hurricane deck."

By the time *Pacific* reached her destination, all the paint was burnt off her smoke stack.

The lake presented defeats and victories for Campbell. It was the destruction of *Manitoulin* that brought *Asia* to Georgian Bay. *Manitoulin* was built in Owen Sound during the winter of 1879-80. The line between Collingwood and Sault Ste. Marie was primarily in service to the bustling lumber industry along the North Shore. In May of 1882, the engine of *Manitoulin* caught fire. Captain Campbell and Chief Engineer William Lockerbie drove her full speed onto the beach at Manitowaning. Once she ran aground, the water was shallow enough that passengers could wade to shore safely. Some passengers ignored orders, panicked, and jumped over-board. This tragic misfortune resulted in eleven deaths. Lockerbie's death grip on the throttle got the ship grounded in six minutes. She was a mile out when fire was discovered. Lockerbie was rewarded with a silver watch for bravery. It would seem that Captain Campbell was rewarded with a ship other than *Asia*, which would replace the burned-out *Manitoulin*.

The Great Northern Transit Company sailed *Asia*, *Emerald* and *Northern Belle* out of Collingwood three times weekly. The steamers were not the finest on the lakes, but they were reported to be "as good as the company can afford". *Asia* was a wooden steam powered vessel with a trim hull, 26-foot beam over 136 feet of keel. She was built in 1873 at St. Catharines. In 1882 she was brought to Georgian Bay to service the lumber trade route formerly ran by *Manitoulin*.

Every Monday, Wednesday and Saturday she left Collingwood at 4 p.m. for the Sault and the North Shore.

Offices of the Great Northern Transit Company in Collingwood as they appeared in 1893, Huron St. Collingwood Museum Collection

Thursdays and Saturdays passengers had an opportunity for a direct route to Parry Sound. The crew was from all around the lakes. Young Arthur Watts of Collingwood, middle son of William and Susan Watts, was a cabin boy aboard the *Asia*.

Arthur's older brothers Matthew, William and George were likely at work in the boat yard. His whole life revolved around the bay. He would have been provided with the same introductory apprenticeship to boat building as his brothers: hours of his boyhood spent in the boat house, smelling of oakum and learning from the expert. The job of cabin boy aboard *Asia* would have came easy for Arthur. Captain Campbell lived nearby and was a partner in the Transit company. "Black Pete" and William were also members of Masonic Lodge in Collingwood, and both attended rescue operations together on the Bay. Arthur was no doubt a suitable candidate for the job of cabin boy of his own accord. He would have had more sailing hours under his belt at the age of 16 than a great deal of other young men in the community.

Arthur left on *Asia* on its regular run from Collingwood, September 13, 1882.

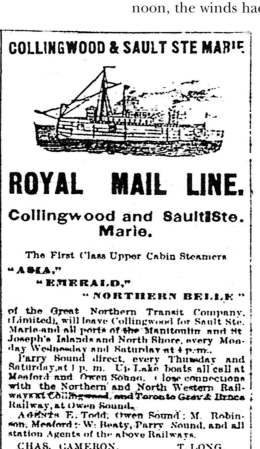

Skies were clear and no warning of a storm was evident. There was little wind when *Asia* left the dock, but by midnight a moderate wind began. By morning, the barometer was dropping steadily and the sky turned grey. Just before noon, the winds had increased to 55 miles an hour, heavy cloud descended and the worst storm in memory was about to begin. The day and date were soon to be remembered by everyone.

It was *Emerald* that caused the greatest tension when the blow stirred up the Bay. *Asia* was considered to be the safer boat of the fleet. That sense of security soon changed to terror when the Captain of *Minnehaha* arrived in town about 9 p.m. and announced the loss of the steamer. By midnight, the wires at the telegraph office were flashing with break-neck speed. Crowds of people gathered at the telegraph office, and along the docks. The weather was still most unpleasant, but the need to gather and confirm the rumours outweighed the intensity of the storm. It wasn't long until only two survivors were reported. Arthur was not one of them.

It's inconceivable to imagine what was going on at the Watts home that night. William likely got the news first. He was a veteran sailor. He'd been on the Lakes when the gales came along. He knew how bad they could get. As a member of the crew who went on rescue missions, he saw first hand what happened to ships when things went wrong and what happened to people who had the misfortune to be sailing at the wrong time.

Any father would be silently hoping the reports were wrong about the two surviving passengers, thinking surely there must be more survivors. William Watts would have known whatever terrible events transpired on the Bay were done and nothing he could do would change the result. The weather was still too severe for him to even attempt to go out.

Northern Belle was already dispatched from Parry Sound and 'Black Pete' Campbell set out in the tug *Mary Ann* to search for bodies. As the finest sailors Collingwood could offer left the harbour, countless others were arriving. They came by train and by ship to wait for news of their loved ones and to wait for bodies to be delivered to port, and take them home for burial. The wreck of *Asia* was the topic of conversation on every street corner, in every house and church. The Great Northern Exhibition's Agricultural Fair was to begin in Collingwood, but the usual festive celebrations were hardly taken note of.

The individual stories began to emerge from the overall magnitude of the disaster. Steve Carter and John McDougall served as steward and purser respectively. Both had served under 'Black Pete' earlier in the year aboard the *Manitoulin*. They survived the flames that engulfed and levelled the hull to the waterline, but they would not survive this one. McDougall had even announced to his wife one day before *Asia* left port that he wouldn't sail another season. His health was failing and it was time to retire. Prophetically it was indeed his last season.

Northern Belle was the first to steam into the port of Collingwood with bodies from the wreck. Her flags were half mast and she appeared almost without a sound, the engines as quiet as could be. There were no sounds from the crew of the *Belle*, no hurrying to tie her mooring ropes. The sight the crew were greeted with was equally as disturbing, a community in mourning. Masses of people, huddling together, holding on to each other, hoping to give a proper burial to their friends and loved ones, while still grasping a shred of hope for their safety.

Only a few were let on board. The *Belle* brought in the only male survivor, 17-year-old Duncan A. Tinkiss. His eloquent account of the accident was the information that hundreds awaited.

Tinkiss reported that everyone was served breakfast at 7:30 a.m. Thursday morning. The wind was blowing heavily, but according to Tinkiss, "No one apprehended any danger whatsoever." Many passengers went back to their births, and by 11 a.m. the ship was rolling. Tinkiss' uncle, also on board, yelled at him, "Dunc jump up, the boat is doomed!"

Tinkiss, his uncle and many others rushed to the upper deck. Hurricane winds were rolling the waves as high as mountains. The majority of the passengers were on the upper deck in short order. The sight of the waves and the rolling of the ship left little doubt of the fate which awaited

MISS C. A. MORRISON,
The only lady surviver of the ill-fated "Asia," wrecked Sept. 14th, 1882.

Cor. King & Yonge Sts.
TORONTO.

Christy Ann Morrison's studio portrait after the Asia *was lost. These cards were used to raise funds for Miss Morrison*
Collingwood Museum Collection

them. Most fell to their knees, praying, crying for mercy and deliverance. The cries were beyond heart-rending. Tinkiss ran back to his cabin for a life preserver. Captain Savage and his crew were not to be seen, but orders to throw the cargo overboard were heard above the winds. Below the deck, *Asia's* cargo was added to the boiling waters. Horses, lumber equipment, winter supplies–all were tossed over. The horses made a horrific, sickening sound. Much of the freight was reportedly stored on the main deck and even some on the hurricane deck. This deadly decision left her holds without weight and top-heavy decks. Nobody dared lower the life boats. There would have been no point in subjecting them to the raging sea and risking losing them too. Recognizing the helplessness of the situation, Tinkiss said, "For a long half hour, we stood there."

Asia fell into the trough of a wave and the engines failed to respond to the commands at the helm. One monstrous wave struck and *Asia* was on her side. The death cries of those dumped into Georgian Bay's waters were a sound Tinkiss would never forget. Christy Ann Morrison, the only other survivor, rarely spoke about it. Tinkiss jumped from the hurricane deck of the ship into one of *Asia's* metallic life boats. The steamer sunk beneath the waves in short order.

The life boat also tipped, dumping all of its frenzied occupants into the water. The flotation tanks ensured it rolled upright again, but too many clung to the boat's side. Recognizing the boat was overcrowded,

Tinkiss made his way to another boat. This was the Captain's boat. In it were Savage and his mates, a few lumbermen and young Arthur Watts. By the time Tinkiss arrived, he noted that Arthur "was dying and was being supported by one of the men, when a wave washed him overboard." It was the last anyone would see of the young cabin boy.

Tinkiss later attributed his survival, and that of Christy Ann Morrison's, to their attempts to sit and hang on to ropes at the bow and stern of the life boat, trying to avoid being impacted by the gunnels as it turned. Their youth didn't hurt them either. Some reports suggest that the Captain and his crew were already so exhausted by trying to keep *Asia* afloat and dumping freight, that there was no energy left to sustain them in an open boat.

The eventual sight of land led to joyous choruses of "Pull for the Shore Sailor" and "In the Sweet By and By". The Mate and Captain quietly passed away, never living to actually set foot on the land they were so close to.

Four days after *Asia* wrecked and the weather cleared, William set out with a small crew on one of his own sail boats to find his son. Matthew set out in another boat in search of his brother. The rest of his family was left home to wait, wonder and watch the still unpredictable weather. William's boat was stopped at Western Islands due to lack of wind. 'Black Pete' Campbell came along in his tug *Mary Ann* and towed him to Parry Sound. The wind appeared with a vengeance and held the the veteran captain and expert boat builder in port till day break. By Tuesday they took their boats to a place where bodies

were discovered. Watts took his sailing boat and explored in one direction, Campbell in the other.

Watts and his son Matthew scoured the small islands in their sail boats from the Minx to Pointe au Baril. All they came up with were two chairs from *Asia,* a bag of flour and pieces of scattered wreck. Captain Campbell picked up *Asia's* piano and some carpet. There was no sign of Arthur.

On Wednesday, William and Matthew Watts returned without success. The Collingwood paper noted William was 'disappointed'. That wouldn't have begun to describe his grief. The same day William arrived without Arthur's body, the *Northern Belle* was unloading the dead on the dock at Collingwood, returning them to their families and loved ones for burial. A grim sight, but a final task that Watts would have been thankful to carry out.

Watts would venture out again in a couple of days, but would return without his son. Captain Campbell said, "Bodies with preservers on may be found, but looking for them is a similar task to searching for a needle in a five acre field and equally hopeful." Campbell would have been a welcome sight for Watts as he carried out the sickening task of searching for Arthur. As neighbours, friends and fellow mariners, they would have comforted each other. 'Black Pete', with his zest for life and the sea, would now see this as the worst navigation season ever, as the captain of the burned–out *Manitoulin,* and now as an owner of the navigation company that operated *Asia*. One can only imagine what they said to each other on the Bay.

An inquiry into the disaster at Parry Sound ruled that there was "insufficient equipment on the boats, and that had those boats been properly supplied with oars and other equipment they might have weathered the storm". The coroner reported that Captain Savage and his mates died of exposure in an open boat, with a lack of oars and nothing to bail the boat with. An unknown person or persons were guilty of manslaughter, according to the jury.

Collingwood's inquiry denounced the style of *Asia*. James E. Evans, a Collingwood hardware merchant, told the inquiry that *Asia* was "one of the worst old canal model of boat. Her upper works from her load-line to her cabin top were not proportioned to the boat's stability; her cabins were too high and she was too much top-hampered. He thought the old canal style of vessel to be unfit for sailing on Georgian Bay, as they were only built to hold a large amount of freight with the least draught of water, their stability being neglected for stowage capacity. The peculiar course taken by steamers while navigating on the Georgian Bay, namely, nearly due north and south, exposed them to more risk on account of the prevailing direction of the winds being east and west, causing them to take the seas broadside. If these canal boats would ply on the waters they were first constructed for, namely, between Montreal and points west of the Welland canal, he thought there would be fewer accidents, for on that route they get the wind either ahead or astern, and there were plenty of harbours to run into, and their time on open waters was limited."

Toronto Daily Mail, October 3, 1882

A few days later, Captain Scott made a similar condemnation on the canal style of boat for Georgian Bay, and suggested they were little more than 'floating coffins'. In defense of the crew, Scott did say that even seasoned sailors were unaware of all the rocks and shoals on the Bay, and nothing short of a mishap would make them apparent.

With all the testimonies heard, the inquest at Collingwood rendered the following verdict: "That the loss of the *Asia* was due to an unprecedented storm which prevailed on the Georgian Bay on the 14th of September last and through narrow judgment on the part of the captain in leaving Presque Isle with the reading of the barometer exceedingly low.

That the Board of Steamboat Inspectors are indirectly to blame for the loss of lives in not notifying the collector of Customs at Collingwood to detain the *Asia* until a new certificate was granted or refused her. We also find from the evidence produced that the *Asia* was in a good state of repair and as far as repairs go, seaworthy. From the evidence produced we do not consider the old Welland canal style of propellers suitable for lake navigation, on account of their bluffness fore and aft, causing them to draw water after them, thereby rendering them difficult to steer in bad weather, especially on the local routes, where the quantity of freight varies from one to three or four hundred tons. We also condemn them for the slightness of their construction, and the height of their upper works. We also condemn the practice of granting certificates to steamboats to carry more passengers than they have life-saving apparatus for, and recommend that all passenger steamers be compelled to carry life-boats and life-rafts sufficient to save all the passengers and crew they are allowed by law to carry, and would also strongly recommend that all captains and mates of all vessels, steam and sail, be subjected to a strict examination before they be allowed to hold such positions. In conclusion, we would suggest that as far as practicable, a list of passengers from the principal ports of embarkation be kept on shore."

Asia would be the catalyst for major changes for aids to inland navigation. For the Watts family, the loss of *Asia* would always be a reminder of the loss of a son and a brother. Arthur's name would be the first to be chiselled out on the family tombstone. The stone was carved. The family picked a plot on a hill in the cemetery in the shade of nearby Maple Trees. Only his name and the date "1884" were recorded, Arthur was never buried there. Georgian Bay never gave him up.

This folk song was later written about the disaster, and mentions the cabin boy, Arthur Watts.

Loud raged the dreadful tumult
And stormy was the day,
When the *Asia* left the harbour
To cross the Georgian Bay.

One hundred souls she had on board,
Likewise a costly store;
But on this trip this gallant ship
Sank to rise no more.

With three and thirty shanty-men
So handsome, stout and brave
Were bound for Collins Inlet,
But found a watery grave.

The men cried, "Save the Captain",
As the waters round him raged;
"Oh no", cried he,"ne'er think of me,
Till all on board are saved".

The cabin boy next passed away,
So young, so true, so brave;
His parents weep while his body sleeps
In Georgian's watery grave.

I'll ne'er forget McDougall
Which was his honoured name,
He immortalized gallant deeds
and hands them down to fame.

And likewise Billy Christie,
With his newly wedded bride,
Were bound for Manitoulin,
Where the parents did reside.

"Oh, had we only left his boat
Last eve at Owen Sound;
Oh, Willie dear, why came we here
To in these waters drown?"

Out in the deep, they're fast asleep,
Their earthly trials are o'er;
Out on the beach their bones will bleach
Along the Georgian shore.

Of all the souls she had on board
Two only are alive;
Miss Morrison and Tinkiss
who only did survive.

Miss Morrison and Tinkiss,
Those names I'll ne'er forget;
Protected by a life boat
which five times did upset.

Around each family circle
How sad the news to hear;
The foundering of the *Asia*,
Left sounding in each ear.

A regatta at the Gorge, Victoria B.C., Queen's birthday 1899. A variety of small craft, row boats and launches can be seen. This photo was sent east to Collingwood by Capt. Wm. Watts to friend David Williams, editor of the Collingwood Enterprise Bulletin *and secretary of the early museum, the* Huron Institute.
Collingwood Museum Collection

9 WATTS & TROTT

FROM COLLINGWOOD TO COAL HARBOUR

*No army can withstand
the strength of an idea
whose time has come*

Victor Hugo, 1802–1885

From personal and business relationships established in the rapidly growing, cosmopolitan town of Collingwood of the 1870's, two of its native sons would begin a trek. The adventure would take them through unexplored bush, forays into Hudson Bay, travel through the virgin prairie, eventually making their way to the young city of Vancouver.

Edward Trott was a member of Collingwood's premier furniture building family. In the late 1800's, furniture makers in any community were also the undertakers. Who better to make a fine oak box for eternal rest than a skilled cabinet maker? Edward Trott grew up around wood workers and finely finished products.

William Watts Jr., brought up in the family tradition of boat building, was the second son of pioneer boat builder William Watts. With a wealth of knowledge on the business operations and management of the Collingwood Yard, young William set out as an accomplished boat builder.

Whether by chance or design, William Jr. and Ed Trott took the opportunity to take an expedition to the head of the lakes. They acted as guides, boat builders and repairmen. The journey took six months. By the fall of 1884 they arrived at Port Arthur.

William found work sailing aboard a small, two-masted schooner named *Annie E. Foster*. She carried 50 to 60 thousand feet of lumber, and Watts was one of a crew of 3[1]. For the next three years, Watts and Trott made Port Arthur their home. The pair established a boat building business on northern Lake Superior's shores. This was a busy port. Supplies for the Canadian Pacific Railway's new wave of construction meant materials were shipped through this region on their trek west.

After three years of operation in Port Arthur, the pair built their last boat for

1. Captain William Watts Jr. to James Barry, February 12, 1939

A.P. Low's Geological Survey in 1887. It was a 30-foot mackinaw, according to Watts, and it was delivered by rail and portage to James Bay after a two–and–a–half month journey. Watts then spent one summer sailing the boat for Low.

Watts & Trott began an adventure-filled trek across the Canadian north en route to Vancouver. Recalling the expedition, Watts later noted, "I arrived in Vancouver in December 1888, having just finished an overland voyage to James Bay and Hudson Bay the year before. A book could be written of great interest of the events that transpired on that memorable voyage. I will not comment on what happened for the balance of the winter." [2]

The two boat builders were greeted with roses blooming at Christmas, an awesome sight for a couple of 'easterners'. They agreed that a better class of light boats was needed for the region. Only one other boat builder had set up shop on the shores of the new city, Andy Linton. Linton was primarily building boats to service the fish trade at the time. The opportunities were endless.

Watts & Trott wasted no time getting down to business. They built a prototype varnished lapstrake skiff. While primarily for their own personal use, it was also a showcase for their building talents. "Trott put a

Large sailing craft under construction at the Vancouver operation.
City of Vancourver Archives BO. P. 176#3 N.492

beautiful furniture finish," on the boats according to his partner. Their efforts were not in vain.

Captain Foreman from Nanaimo took notice of their prototype. He was renting boats commercially, and made

---

2. Autobiography of Captain William Watts, Pioneer,
   City of Vancouver Archives

a business trip to interview the pair. He didn't leave their Water Street operation before ordering 25 new boats. This magnitude of an order for an unknown builder was virtually unheard of. The first test of the new 'Watts & Trott Boat Building Company' was underway.

"I can assure you, as time was the essence of that contract, working hours did not enter into it in any way whatsoever. Sixteen or eighteen hours a day was ordinary, and did we have disgruntled neighbours owing to the noise we made?" [3]

Putting in long work hours to fill their orders, Watts and Trott also constructed a craft to compete in an upcoming rowing event. In a successful effort to showcase the versatility of the fledgling firm, a light 20-foot outrigger boat was designed and built. Watts proceeded to get in shape and row the vessel himself.

William was no stranger to rowing competitions in Collingwood, or the winner's circle for that matter. He put himself on a rigid training schedule, two times a day for three weeks. William recalls, "I got so thin I was ashamed to look at myself ."

His idea paid off. Watts won his first race on the West Coast by a healthy margin. The victory was followed by many orders for 40-foot outriggers by other regional rowing clubs.

The needs of the growing salmon industry required the construction of countless fishing boats. With only

The flourishing salmon industry on the Fraser River–a morning haul. National Archives of Canada PA31664

one other commercial builder, Andy Linton, servicing this field, an eastern boat builder with deep foundations in the Great Lakes fishing trade had a chance to make a significant contribution to the traditions of the fishing industry on the west coast.

The Collingwood Skiff, or mackinaw designs, that were used with great success on the Great Lakes were about to be introduced to the west coast fishery. The seaworthy characteristics of the Collingwood Skiffs and their application for fishing, made the Skiff well adapted to the West Coast salmon fishery . Watts and Trott would produce the double-ended, clinker-built Skiff in huge numbers. Upon their arrival in Vancouver, the salmon industry was being serviced by flat-bottomed skiffs. Watts recalls they were "sharp bow and square transom, flaring

3. Autobiography of Captain William Watts, Pioneer,
   City of Vancouver Archives

A young Captain William Watts Jr. and his bride Emily Leckie. Emily was the daughter of John Leckie, successful Toronto marine supplier.
City of Vancouver Archives PORT. P. 318 N.1230

sides, 18 to 20 feet long, 5 foot beam. Some had centre-boards and single sprit sails, and others just oars."[4] The average price of these boats in 1888 was $50 to $65.

Then Watts & Trott gained the attention of the fishermen by producing something dramatically different. A 24-foot mackinaw was built and raced in a regatta on the coast. It was quickly sold to a swordfish fisherman. On the heels of this transaction, the design became very popular. The designs that were known on the lakes as a Collingwood Skiff would now adopt a new regional name, the Columbia River Skiff.

The firm's largest order on record was placed by Henry Bell Irving, a prominent British Columbian Salmon packer. Bell Irving ordered 100 boats to be delivered in one season. The boats were 25 feet long, 7 foot beam, 28 inches deep. All were equipped with a centreboard, main sail and jib. Recalling the building of the 100 boats, Watts reports:

"I built them bottom up on a solid mold and turned out one every day complete. Most of them were carvel built, and the reason for their popularity is good sea boat and

Certificate of Superiority awarded to Watts & Trott for design and construction of a boat. Presented in San Francisco in 1895. Bill Watts Collection

so easy to fish up a net in hauling them into any kind of a sea...and now all this changed (when) Japanese came here in droves and began building their own boats and fishing, and all now have power boats of various sizes from 25 to 35 feet and they did not get far away from the Mackinaw stern."[5]

Salmon were not the only fish Watts boats would be used for. In 1893, Watts & Trott "built the first halibut fishing boats for the Pacific Halibut Company."[6] When the boats were supplied, the fishermen caught their halibut in a manner of hours. By the late 1930's, halibut fishermen travelled several hundred miles to catch enough fish to make it worth their while.

By 1895, the floating advertisements for Watts & Trott were numerous around the coast, the Columbia and Fraser River. The duo took a rowboat and exhibited it at the Industrial Exposition in San Francisco. Their rowboat earned them a "Certificate of Superiority", the highest award

---

4. Captain William Watts Jr. to James Barry October 1, 1937.

5. Captain William Watts Jr. to James Barry, October 1, 1937.
6. Autobiography of Captain William Watts, pioneer 1888.
   City of Vancouver Archives

given for an exhibition in their class at the show.

Trott's health was failing, and the San Francisco weather was thought to do him good. Watts came back to British Columbia and ran the stern wheeler *Telephone* from Harrison Hot Springs, transporting miners and their supplies to the gold fields on their way to Dawson. "I made more money than the miners," boasts Watts. *Telephone* was a wooden stern wheeler, 74 feet long, 14'6" beam and 3'6" deep. She plied the waters between New Westminster and Port Douglas, at the north end of Harrison Lake.[7]

Trott moved to Calgary and forged a partnership with his brother Samuel in the City's first pharmacy. Watts bought out his share of the Watts & Trott Boat Building Company, and carried on without his cabinet maker friend from Collingwood. Their colourful expedition across the continent together had come to an end. Watts continued to build boats under his own name.

7. Affleck, Edward. *Affleck's List of Sternwheelers Plying the Inland Waters of British Columbia.* Alexander Nicolls Press. 1992

Stern wheeler Telephone *seen parked at Harrison Hot Springs. Captain William Watts Jr. ran* Telephone *from New Westminster to head of Harrison Lake, taking miners to the Klondike gold fields.*
Vancouver Maritime Museum Collection

Ruth was a naptha launch purchased by William Watts. He can be seen sitting at the stern. Ruth is clearly decked out for a festive occasion.
Vancouver Public Library, #19877

1926 aerial view of Vancouver's Coal Harbour shows a hub of boat building activity. Photo: RCAF. City of Vancouver Archives No. CVA 392 918

As if to announce that he was still in business after the departure of his friend and partner Ed Trott, William Watts took out a sizable ad in Henderson's 1901 Directory for the City of Vancouver. The Watts & Trott Boat Yard had undergone a change. Watts would carry on with fervour.

At the turn of the century, Coal Harbour was well–populated with boat builders. The 1901 advertisement echoes the mantle of the Collingwood operation, "All kinds of Pleasure Yachts and Skiffs." Anything was possible.

Change also meant a new location for Watts. As the Canadian Pacific Railway was continuing its progress, the fill created from the laying of the rail lines forced Watts to move from his operation outside the piling of the C.P.R. main line between Cambie and Abbott street to the foot of Gilford Street at Coal Harbour. For the first two years at that location he operated simply as his advertisement suggests, "William Watts Shipbuilder". By the spring of 1902, he incorporated the company as the Vancouver Shipyards with $20,000 in capital with shares of $25.

Soon after he branched out on his own, Watts decided to try his hand at broom making, which he did in the shipyard on

I know not what the world will think of my labours, but to myself it seems as if I have been as a child playing on the seashore; now finding some prettier pebble or more beautiful shell than my companion, while the unbounded ocean of truth lay undiscovered before me.

Sir Isaac Newton, 1642–1727

WM. WATTS
Ship and Boat Builder

Tugs, Stern Wheelers,
Steam Yachts & Launches
SCOWS AND LIGHTERS.

Racing Shells, Canoes, Oars and Paddles a specialty.   All kinds of repair work promptly attended to.

1901 Georgia and Gilford Sts.

VANCOUVER, B. C.

1901 Henderson's Directory

Gilford and Georgia Street. He proclaims to have made the first corn broom in Vancouver in 1901. The British Columbia Broom and Brush Works operated for only a year and a half. Eastern brooms made by prisoners were far cheaper for the consumer, and Watts' little broom producing a quality broom. The corn was imported to Vancouver from Oklahoma, the tools were brought in from Chicago and an expert broom manufacturer was brought on site from New York. Looking back on the efforts he made to launch this company Watts said, "You see I was calculating to turn out a good article however, I wrote it down to experience." [1] This is the spirit he brought to boat construction, always calculating to turn out a good article.

In this early picture of the Vancouver Shipyard, Captain William Watts can be seen standing outside the winch at the top of a marine railway with his hands on his hips. The photograph is early enough to show a group of men standing in the doorway flaunting a collection of brooms, still available for any willing customer.

Brooms failed Watts, but boats never did. In the decades to follow after the establishment of the

Vancouver Shipyard, the golden area of pleasure cruisers and yachts was born. The Collingwood operation seemed to have a variety of boats for work or commercial purposes at the heart of their operation, and the Vancouver Shipyard may be remembered more for opulent, floating show pieces. Clearly, both yards produced any kind of vessel the customer ordered.

Maple Leaf was one of Watts' crowning accomplishments, and still in sail today. She was built in 1904 for Alexander McLaren, a wealthy British Columbia lumber baron. Even before she splashed into the waters at Coal Harbour,

'The Vancouver Shipyard. Boats, Scows, Steamers and Vessels Built and Repaired. Oars Manufactured. Boats Bought and Sold. Marine Surveyor. Capt. W. Watts, Manager.'
Vancouver Public Library

1. Autobiography of Captain William Watts, pioneer 1888, City of Vancouver Archives, Vancouver British Columbia.

This view of the Vancouver shipyard not only shows a sizable staff, but a diversity of boats. Small boats at the right prepare to be planked in the Carvel style, probably for the fish trade. The larger Forrest Queen *is under construction at the left. Captain Watts is in the centre with his arms folded.* Vancouver Public Library

The variety of craft in the yard, in the slip, under construction and hanging from the rafters shows their diversity on the west coast. Vancouver Public Library

A tug, racing shell and a few sailboats at the Vancouver Shipyards
Vancouver Public Library Collection

Collingwood Old Boys' Association

COLLINGWOOD, ONT., FEB. 23, 1903

DEAR SIR,

Many of the sons of Collingwood have gone forth from the old town to better their fortunes in other spheres, and are scattered throughout all parts of the North American Continent. Those of us who have remained at home and watched the old town develop into a thriving business centre, have not lost sight of those old boys, but have marked with pleasure and pride that the great majority of them occupy positions of trust and responsibility in the various places in which they have located, and are on the high road to success and fortune, many indeed, having already achieved them.

Collingwood in the 50's

The formation of an Old Boys' Association has long been a cherished idea among the old boys, both at home and abroad, and this idea has at length crystallized into fact, and an Association has been perfected with the above executive officers. It is the intention to have a grand reunion of Collingwood Old Boys some time during the ensuing summer, when it is expected a large concourse of former residents will gather together with their wives, sisters and sweethearts, and renew old associations in the old town.

Any person, without regard to age, who has at any time resided for two years in the Town of Collingwood, or its immediate vicinity, is entitled to membership in the Association, the fee for which has been fixed at the nominal sum of fifty cents.

Collingwood in 1902

Vancouver 1919. Vancouver was a popular area for many of Collingwood's men to re-establish themselves. They met frequently to reminisce about the 'old town.' Pictured from left to right (standing) James Lightheart, J. McCormick, John Storey, William Lightheart. (Seated) Thomas McCormick, Capt. W.A.Clark and Capt. William Watts Jr.
Collingwood Museum Collection

The 'Old Boys' referred to any one who left Collingwood and settled elsewhere. This 1903 brochure shows the spirit of the club and their reunions held in Collingwood and anywhere the Old Boys gathered. Watts Collection

Maple Leaf was being hailed as the costliest yacht ever built, with a price tag of $12,000. No expense or modern convenience was spared. Teak wood lined the interior and the electric lights, a first for a yacht in Coal Harbour, were supplied by a dynamo. McLaren sailed her locally at the Royal Vancouver Yacht Club and through the Gulf Islands on leisurely social cruises. By the time War broke out, McLaren was forced to sell her lead keel to support the war effort. By 1916, he sold *Maple Leaf*, no longer a yacht, but a fish packer.

After 57 years of fishing under the name *Constance B.* and *Parma*, *Maple Leaf* showed little signs of being a luxury vessel. Her rigging, decks and cabins had undergone significant modifications. In 1973, the Canadian Government acquired her as part of a halibut buy-back program. Neil Varcoe surveyed the boat for a prospective customer thinking it looked as if it were a sailing vessel at one time. Despite the massive changes, her hull was still intact and sound. New owner Brian Falconer spared no expense in bringing her back to being a glorious yacht, worthy of being any yacht club's flagship. She is now gracing the Pacific shores again. Pleasure sailors can now enjoy *Maple Leaf* on a variety of cruises offered by operator Brian Falconer.

The Vancouver Shipyard had a broad customer base. Life boats, tenders, rowboats and other small craft were produced in great number by the yard. These often

Maple Leaf *shortly after she was built in 1904.*
Vancouver Maritime Museum Collection

nameless, personal use craft were simply overshadowed by the luxurious cruisers that the yard had a reputation for.

Watts self-righting, self-bailing life boat, built for the Banfield Creek Life Saving Station, was the first of its kind at Vancouver. This massive, carvel vessel was propelled only by oars.

Recalling the variety of craft produced by the yard, Watts says:

"I built 3 fifty-foot gas boats, two to be used for fish packers and the other to be used as a pleasure boat, all the same model hulls named *Adam, Eve* and *Beatrice*. That same year I built for Joe McDowell, the *Jessie Mack*, sixty five foot tow boat. Then I built a power schooner *Fort MacPherson*, power schooner *Chief Zebassi*, and *Chief*

Right:
Maple Leaf *converted into the fish packer* Parma. Vancouver Maritime Museum Collection

Below:
Maple Leaf *returned to a glorious yacht. She is still sailing Pacific Waters.* Vancouver Maritime Museum Collection

A finely dressed crew for an exquisite yacht. Vancouver Maritime Museum Collection

Capt. William Watts Jr. stands behind his self-bailing, self-righting boat built for the Banfield Creek Life Saving Station. City of Vancouver Archives BO. P.177 N.479

Skugaid for Prince Rupert Cold Storage Co., built power schooner *Nigalik* for the North West Traders in their Arctic Work. The largest boat we built was the *Teco* to the order of A. J. T. Taylor & Associates, 135 feet long. We also built a number of tugs and scows for B.C. Packers and other canners and many other fine yachts and commercial boats of all kinds, too numerous to mention." [2]

The *Fort MacPherson* was the first power schooner into the Arctic circle on the Pacific side. It was one of a number of boats built for Hudson's Bay Company by Watts.

Linda, a 52-foot steam screw was built in 1904 for John Leckie of Toronto, a well-known merchant for marine provisions and Thomas Kinnelt of Vancouver, an accountant. John Leckie was also William Watts' father-in-law. *Linda* was sold later to Canada Fish Products, and then condemned and dismantled by 1912 after a short career. *Linda* and her sister-ship *Edna* were both tugs used for the oilery on the Fraser River.

Watts' Vancouver Shipyard is noted to have been the earliest to "cater to the needs and whims of the honourable members of local yacht clubs and other people able and wanting to join the pleasure boating set." [3] In the period prior to the First World War, a fine collection of impressive power boats were turned out by Captain Watts. The *Rhinegold*, still gracing the port of Vancouver, was the epitome of cruising when it was launched in

2. Autobiography of Captain William Watts, pioneer 1888.
   City of Vancouver Archives.

3. Vassilopoulos, Peter. *Antiques Afloat*, Panorama Publications Ltd. 1980

Chief Skugaid *was built by the Vancouver Shipyard for the Prince Rupert Cold Storage Company.* Vancouver Maritime Museum Collection

Nigalik *was a power schooner built for work in the Arctic.* Vancouver Maritime Museum Collection

Workers leave Nigalik *and go exploring across Arctic ice.* Nigalik *means 'goose'.* Vancouver Maritime Museum Collection

1911. She was built for Theophilus Maxwell Davies, a Vancouver businessman. He sold *Rhinegold* after one year to Dr. Glen Campbell. By 1923, Colonel Colin Ferrie had purchased her for $2,500. Colonel Ferrie sailed her for almost 6 decades. Her longevity is due to incredibly sturdy construction. Planks are 1 5/8th cedar below the water-line, and fir above. The 2" oak ribs are on 8" centres. Upon launch, she was fitted out with a Buffalo 20 hp engine. *Rhinegold's* hull is an evolution from some of the early fishing boats on the coast. She is double ended, and narrow beamed. Like many of the fishing boats on Georgian Bay, she cruises along at low speeds with very little wake.

Another surviving treasure from Watts yard is the *Wanderer*. She was launched as *Cora May* in 1924, built

Captain William Watts notes that the Fort MacPherson *was his first power schooner.*
Vancouver Maritime Museum Collection

The 135 foot Teco, *the largest boat to have graced the ways at the Vancouver Shipyard.*
Vancouver Maritime Museum Collection

The schooner Casco *was owned by author Robert Louis Stevenson. Although built in San Francisco in 1878, she was on the ways at the Vancouver Shipyards for repair. Capt. William Watts Jr. said she was one of the finest vessels ever on the ways.* City of Vancouver Archives. BO. P.264. N.169

from some of the lumber left from the *Empress of Japan* which was scrapped at Vancouver. Captain Watts was no stranger to reusing lumber. When the Hudson's Bay Company steamer *Beaver* was wrecked at Vancouver, Watts recalls:

"When I arrived at Vancouver, the famous *Beaver* was lying on her beam ends on Prospect Point, abandoned by the Underwriters, and I believe I was the first man to begin dismantling her and still have some souvenirs of her." [4]

Cora May was purchased by National Defense for submarine patrol during the Second World War. Her charming hull was covered in camouflage, hiding her sleek appearance. She was later purchased by a private citizen, and after a great deal of renovations became the flagship of the Royal Vancouver Yacht club. Still afloat as *Wanderer*, the timbers which first formed portions of her hull from the *Empress of Japan* are well over a century old.

Chemona was built by the Vancouver Shipyard for Captain Watts' own use. Her spacious carvel hull was used for private expeditions and cruises. Aside from his treks to the hunt clubs of the region, Watts was a visible part of the Vancouver social scene. He enjoyed visits to the opera house, the rowing club and was given the job of Deputy Harbour Master of Coal Harbour in 1911. Later, in 1930, he was given the title of 'Honourary' Harbour Master.

In the same fashion as William Watts learned the finer points of boat building, his sons Harold and Clarence were exposed to shipyard work. William was as stubborn as he was colourful, and his sons felt a calling toward

work other than boat building. Clarence worked as a machinist in the shop, but according to his son Jack, "He was never really given the option" to carry on. Clarence went on to a career in real estate. His older brother Harold also worked for his father. He went on to study chemistry at the University of British Columbia which led to a career in chemical engineering, a far cry from boat building.

As the depression loomed, the demand for opulent pleasure craft was in decline. By 1929, Captain William Watts, one of Vancouver's most lively pioneers was 67, and had seen more of the great expanse of Canada than most. It was time for him to retire. The thirties would bring a decline in the demand for any luxury item, but the Vancouver Shipyard still had a service to offer. Pleasure craft would come back in demand again. Watts was left with no choice but to sell the Vancouver Shipyard. The son of pioneer fish packer Duncan Bell-Irving, partnered with James Hoffar to purchase the firm. They produced a few vessels, including the lovely *Cora Marie*, but the profit margins shrunk drastically. Hoffar and Bell-Irving went bankrupt. By 1933 the Yard had new owners, with 50 employees. Only three years of operation were enjoyed until they too went bankrupt. Former Boeing Aircraft production manager Gilbert Jukes purchased the operation in 1936 and located it on the original site.

With the sale of his shipyard, Captain William Watts was no longer managing one of the earliest boat yards in Vancouver. Mulling over his contributions and accomplishments, he remembers the men who worked under him:

4. Autobiography of Captain William Watts, *City of Vancouver Archives*

Cora May *was used for sub-marine patrol in WW2. She is still sailing today as* Wanderer. Vancouver Public Library

Cora Marie *all decked out for launch day. Seen here still on the ways of the Vancouver Shipyard 1929.* Vancouver Maritime Museum Collection

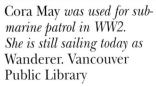

The Cora Marie *was on the ways when Capt. Watts sold the Vancouver Shipyard in 1929.* Vancouver Maritime Museum Collection

CHEMONA

Chemona *in Snug Harbour on Bowen Island Resort, a popular hunting ground for Watts and his pals. A number of Watts small craft are visible behind the impressive* Chemona.
Jack Watts Collection

Watts own vessel Chemona. *Capt. Watts is standing at the left, showing off his hunting trophies.* Jack Watts Collection

Dining saloon below decks was designed for large capacity seating and comfort. The engine room of the Cora Marie, *shows her original power,* National Superior *probably 160 hp.* Vancouver Maritime Museum Collection

The charming Cora Marie, a fine vessel for the Vancouver Shipyard. Cora Marie was the pinnacle of wooden craft construction. **Vancouver Maritime Museum Collection.**

"I have had many apprentices under my supervision and whether from a knowledge of human nature or sheer good luck, I had a wonderful selection and without an exception they have all made good. I tried to be fair with them and keep their respect, and it is a great pleasure to look back and think of the good times we had like one big family. I have been blessed with good health in all these years and now that I am on the shelf, I intend to keep up my hobby (fishing). So old boys, when you retire, get a hobby." [5]

Captain Watts had plenty to keep him busy in retirement. He dabbled in real estate and kept an active social life. Although the property was sold in 1929, family tradition notes that William himself didn't leave the yard until 1930 or 31. It's likely that the old salt couldn't stay away that easy, and stayed on to maintain a level of consistency in construction and service to an elite client base.

Even at 90, he dressed himself in a jacket, tie, hat and walking stick to make his mile long daily excursion on Stanley and Cypress Park. Much of his time he spent talking of his stimulating life. His experiences were indeed unique, but just his telling of them seemed to make them just a little more lively. His enthusiasm to be the first at almost every major event got the best of him at times.

Captain Watts had a good friendship with the City Archivist, Major Matthews. On their many get-togethers, Major Matthews recorded Watts tales. Matthews often corrected Watts.

Watts claimed that his launching of the steamboat *Miramichi* was the first at Vancouver. In his own notes, Matthews writes "not correct, the *Maggie* was built on George Black's platform at Gastown, before 1878". Watts was quick to add that *Miramichi* was the first steamboat built on the Peninsula. One thing even Captain Watts wouldn't claim, was that he was not the first boat builder to set up shop at Vancouver. He never fails to credit builder Andy Linton with that honour. Naturally, he can't resist noting that Linton built primarily work boats, and not the pleasure craft and racing shells churned out by Watts & Trott or the Vancouver Shipyard.

Thankfully for small craft enthusiasts, Watts did feel confident to share his accomplishments in detail with a number of people, and some details of them are available for the telling over half a century later. Watts died at 92 in 1954. His ashes were scattered in the Pacific Ocean. He once noted "I have been associated with the water front so long, I am getting web–footed, so you see, I should not object to being called Barnacle Bill the Sailor." [6]

The Vancouver Shipyard is still in operation and is now the oldest boat building firm in the region. Captain Watts would surely curl his mouth back to a wry smile if he only knew the company he started is the oldest in existence in Vancouver, even if it wasn't the first.

5. Autobiography of Captain William Watts, City of Vancouver Archives, Vancouver, British Columbia

6. Autobiography of Captain William Watts, City of Vancouver Archives, Vancouver, British Columbia

Point Garry *under construction at the Vancouver Shipyard.*
Vancouver Maritime Museum Collection

Silene *of Prince Rupert was involved in the fishing industry. She was built by the Vancouver Shipyard.* Vancouver Public Library, No. 29134

West Vancouver No. 5 *escorting a full cargo of passengers.* Vancouver Maritime Museum Collection

The Vancouver Shipyard just after the retirement of Captain William Watts Jr. According to Bill Watts, grandson of Capt. Watts, his grandfather was still involved in the business until 1931.
Vancouver Public Library, No.11390

Captain William Watts Jr. cruising in Etude, *complete with pillows, umbrella and lights. A suitable retirement pass time for a colourful man of many lakes.* Watts Collection

This overview of Collingwood Harbour, April 27, 1900, shows a busy shipping and boat building port. The Watts & Sons shop can be seen in the centre, to the right of the slip with a number of launches and skiffs in and around the waterfront.
Collingwood Museum Collection

april 27/1900
Collingwood Harbour

INHERITED TRADITIONS

THE SECOND GENERATION

He was the kind of guy everyone liked. He was serious about his work, but Matthew Watts was never too busy to spend some time with his nieces and nephews or joke around with the neighbourhood kids. "Uncle Matt was my favourite," said Reg Watts, "He gave me cigarettes." Others who remember him fondly recall him handing out candy or flashing a mischievous smile.

"When I was a boy of fourteen my father was so ignorant I could hardly stand to have the old man around. But when I got to twenty-one, I was astonished at how much the old man had learned in seven years."

Mark Twain, 1835–1910

Matthew Watts was the oldest child of William and Susan Watts. He was born in MacDuff, County Sligo, Ireland. When his father died in 1905, Matthew was left to manage the boat building operation. Naturally, his brothers were a vital part of the business as well. He was a revered boat builder.

Matthew was able to maintain the solid and diverse customer base established by his father. During his time, the company continued to turn out mackinaws, rowboats, tugs and pleasure craft of all kinds.

For a time, Matthew Watts built boats outside the Watts boat yard at a separate facility. In the region which was used for years as the launch slip for the Collingwood Shipyard, Matthew Watts constructed

Matthew Watts, Manito Lodge #90 Collection

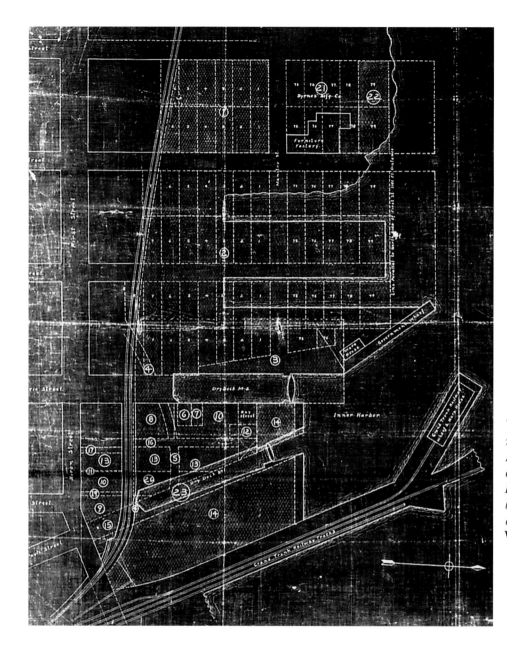

The lot identified as number 6 was owned by Matthew Watts. It occupied 50 ft. by 80 ft. Doherty was his boat building neighbour with area number 7.
Watts Collection

A group of Collingwood men at Collingwood Wharf, 1907.
From left to right: David Williams, T.C.Brown, W.J.Swain, J.G.Noble,
W.R.Roeland and Matthew Watts. Watts Collection

When Matthew Watts managed the company, he operated on the east side of this launch slip, Although the shop is out of this frame, a tug taking shape is visible at the right. A steam tug and a fish boat float in the slip. Watts Collection

larger vessels such as tugs. They were of such a size they had to be constructed outdoors. The demand for tugs by fishermen alone during this time period dictated this move.

In January of 1935, Matthew died in his home on Pine Street in Collingwood. The oldest son, second-generation boat builder and friend to everyone who had the opportunity to make his acquaintance was widely mourned. Matthew operated the boat house for 30 years, and earned a reputation of his own accord. He never married and was not reported to have a lengthy illness at the time of his death.

Matthew Watts also left behind countless small craft of every variety across the continent. As is customary, he was buried under Masonic auspices. He had been a member of the Manito Lodge and had served as Worshipful Master in 1894.

The editor of The *Enterprise-Bulletin,* David Williams, reported his death on the front page of the paper. For Williams, he was not only reporting the passing of a well-known community citizen which he deemed to be newsworthy, but saying goodbye to a good friend. "Collingwood suffered heavily," he noted, and referred to him simply as Matt. "He was a good friend, a true companion and never swayed in his support of that he believed right."

Mira Watts was the family caregiver. Mira, Daisy and Matthew lived in the same house on Pine Street in Collingwood. Mira was a petite and quiet woman who worked to run the household smoothly. As the oldest daughter, she was taught and expected to be a help to her mother and generally adopted a maternal role

Daisy Watts, pictured here in front of her Maple St. Residence c. 1950. McIntyre Family Collection

Miss Minnie Martin hosted a concert in 1890. Daisy Watts is standing in the back row, second from the right. Lizzie Doherty, daughter of boat builder Patrick Doherty is seated in the centre row far left.
Collingwood Museum Collection

with the rest of the family. She never married. When her brother Robert had a daughter, he told his wife she would be named Mira, "because every mother should have a Mira."

Daisy fulfilled a different role. Whether by nature or by choice, she was more independent and outgoing. She was tall and outspoken. Daisy was considered to be quite 'liberated' for a woman of her generation. She had a mind for business and not only performed book keeping tasks for the boat building operation, but held joint power of attorney with Matthew at one time. Daisy Watts was a member of Collingwood's elite. The boat building business had provided well for her, her sister and the rest of their family. Her flamboyant lifestyle, fashionable clothing and parade of new cars meant she was part of a very small percentage of Collingwood women.

Robert

Practically every son had his Captain's papers, and the family stuck together in most endeavours. When Robert Watts left Collingwood, gave up his Canadian citizenship and became a naturalized citizen of the Commonwealth of Pennsylvania in 1899, he was very unpopular at home. To complicate the issue, Robert married Mary North in 1901, a Catholic. Although the wedding was a small one by design, not one member of Robert's family attended. It's difficult to determine the exact reasons why Robert's decisions weren't supported by his family in Collingwood. At the turn of the century, there may have been a general discouragement to anyone marrying outside their

denomination. Although William was certainly no stranger to conflicts between Protestant and Catholics in his native Ireland, he was not remembered for being against either denomination. Perhaps the family had hoped Robert would follow along with his brothers and work in the boat shop in Collingwood. Whatever the reason, his contact with family was infrequent.

Robert was a mariner and a fisherman. It was a life he knew well. He held the title of Chief Engineer on American fishing tug *Silver Spray* and was a member of the International Longshoreman's Association.

In bitter cold March of 1911, the *Silver Spray* left Cleveland for a routine fishing expedition. The Lake grew angry and tossed the fish tug relentlessly, until a valve in the engine room blew and rendered the tug helpless in the teeth of the freezing storm. Watts, called 'Bobby' by his ship mates and friends, removed three bolts off the steam chest in an effort to repair the broken valve, and prevent the tug from capsizing entirely. As the seas raged, water poured into the engine room, and Watts, wearing only overalls and a shirt, pushed on to repair the mechanics of the now–battered tug. In this desperate situation, Watts had to prevent the incoming waters from reaching the boilers and filling the room with scalding steam. Recognizing the additional threat, he detached the engine's eccentric, a cam used in the engine, and tied it to the side of the engine room, to prevent it from striking him as the tug rolled in the fury.

The crew signalled for an hour for assistance at the entrance to the harbour. No rescue effort was launched.

The Government had closed the Life Saving Station at the advice of a district superintendent.

His heroic efforts proved futile. Watts jumped overboard, along with the other six crew members, into Lake Erie's frigid waters. None would survive. Robert Watts left behind his wife and four children.

When the *Silver Spray* was raised by a salvage company, the knot 'Bobby' Watts tied in the engine room was a grim testimony to the events that transpired. In jest, one of the crew members of the salvage operation commented "the fisher fished" as the tug broke the water. He was silenced as the battered hull dripped from every seam, with no evidence of a cabin and the bottom of the hull was all but missing. The next comment to escape the lips of the salvage operator was "that man was a hero".

The United States Government came under attack after the accident for minimalizing the lives and value of mariners and fishermen by closing the Life Saving Station for three months. This move was made to save taxpayers $2,000. In a news account of the disaster, the reporter writes:

> "A crew of seven men who risk their lives a dozen times during the season during the discharge of their duty, are turned adrift during the winter to eat up the amount saved from their season's salary, while fishermen and longshoremen who are engaged at the lake front are left unprotected. If Captain Hansen had assistance to launch his motor boat, he could have gone out to the *Silver Spray* alone and taken off the

> crew....the signals were seen by the authorities ashore, and those men were allowed to drift helplessly on the rocks and die a miserable death after a desperate struggle during which everything to be done to save themselves was tried by them. The treasury department saved $2,000 and lost seven lives, while the War Department is spending $1,000,000 in army manoeuvres to protect property in Mexico. Truly, property seems to be more valuable than human life."

Watts' young family was left alone. "My father never believed in insurance," recalled his oldest daughter Myra. "Just before he came to Cleveland, he took out a $500 policy, that's it."

Mary Watts, Robert's widow, was a strong and determined woman. She entered the work force and was appointed Tipstaff in the Erie Pennsylvania court system by 1922. It was the first time a woman was ever named to the post on a full-time basis. She was tall and statuesque, and many commented if she ever desired to enter the political ring, she would have aspired to any office in the land. She was the kind of a woman who wanted to make it on her own.

Myra, who was almost 8 when her father drowned on the *Silver Spray*, is quick to point out that "those Collingwood Watts never helped my mother", but later cites many occasions where help was offered, but was denied by her mother. "The Watts told my mother they'd raise me and my three brothers and sisters in Collingwood, but she wouldn't have any part of that."

Myra was sent on a train to spend her summers in

Collingwood. From March to October she was exposed to the family of her father. She stayed with George and Leah Watts on Maple Street. Well into her 90's, Myra Watts still smiles thinking of riding Emily Watts bicycle. "I never had a bicycle," she lamented. The lack of a bicycle in her youth was a constant thorn in her side. Without her mother's knowledge, she wrote to her Uncle William in Vancouver and let him know that she didn't have a bicycle, and Emily Watts in Collingwood had a fine one that she could only ride when she visited in the summer. Uncle William sent Myra $100. Her mother was enraged that Myra would ask anybody for help, but the money was kept.

In Collingwood, her Uncle Matthew inquired how much the train ride cost from Erie. He always gave her the $10 fare, and never failed an opportunity to fill her's and every other kids' pockets with candy and treats.

Myra never graced the threshold of the boat building operation in her summers at Collingwood. "Girls just didn't go there," she said. "We did go for sail boat rides to Meaford for a picnic every once in a while, but not very often."

On a visit to Captain Watts in Vancouver, Myra was greeted with the comment, "I didn't know Robert was married, never mind had any children". This comment, likely made in his usual spirit of teasing, only added to her feeling of alienation. Through all the incredible sadness Myra has endured over a long life, she remains intensely proud of her family's heritage, particularly her mother and father.

George

In the Collingwood Collegiate Institute yearbook, George Watts was honoured with a little poem:
"Who can build a boat and make her float?
Webb Watts can!"

Webb, a nickname that followed George throughout his life, worked alongside his brothers at the boat shop. When a few lucky miners hit gold at Rabbit Creek in the Yukon, the old Irish yearning to find the "gold at the end of the rainbow" was ignited. Canadians, Americans and people from around the globe poured into Dawson City.

In 1898, Webb assembled some necessary supplies, a dog team and a few friends for the pilgrimage north-west. An impressive send off was mounted for the hopefuls in front of Collingwood's Grand Central Hotel. Brother Thomas joined in the prospecting too. Between 1907 and 1911, George 'Webb' Watts laid claim to three land grants in the Klondike. Older brother William found another way to strike it rich during the gold rush.

In 1895, William skippered the sternwheeler *Telephone* out of Harrison Hot Springs. For three years, he transported supplies and prospectors closer to the gold fields.

As for Webb, he is credited with some boat building in the Yukon as well as prospecting. Boats used in the Yukon were typically slammed together, flat-bottomed, almost dory-like. Few others were finer built. Men who had never built a boat before tried their luck.

A few Collingwood old timers think they know at least one boat Watts left in the Yukon. "That barge at Lake Lemarge in the poem was built by Watts," claims Ernie

The Grand Central Hotel
corner of Hurontario and Simcoe Streets
Collingwood, Ontario

Many townspeople gathered on January 31, 1898 to bid farewell to several residents who ventured to the Klondike Gold Rush. The local prospectors are Fred A. Johnson, Charlie H. Fair, J. Sanson and George F. Watts. **Collection Collingwood Museum**

Brock, an early employee of W. Watts and Sons.

Robert Service's poem *The Cremation of Sam McGee* tells of two fictitious prospectors battling the elements in Dawson. Sam McGee was actually a bank teller at Dawson. Service used his name but created the story. The barge *Alice May*, which was to be Sam's "cre-ma-tor-eum" was also a fictional name, but many boats and barges lay abandoned around Lake Lemarge. The slip-shod construction methods frequently led to disaster. Whether Watts built a barge at Lake Lemarge or not may never be known. For a few Collingwood old timers, it makes a darn good story.

Webb came back to Collingwood and continued working alongside his brothers. He married Leah Telfer, daughter of a prominent Collingwood biscuit manufacturer and Dry Goods shopkeeper.

Thomas

Thomas Harper Watts followed the migration of his brothers west. Like the rest of the boys, he worked in the Collingwood boat building operation during his youth. Thomas didn't pursue boat building as a career, but was the operator of a fish boat most of his life.

On visits to his brother William in Vancouver, Tom was described as quiet, tall and powerfully built. Northern British Columbia, Prince Rupert and Vancouver were his favourite fishing ports. From Prince Rupert, Thomas ordered a new fish tug from the Vancouver Shipyard, which was of substantial size. The magnitude of the tug was an indication of his years of success as a fisherman.

William and Susan Watts were blessed with 14 children. The younger ones enjoyed a comfortable lifestyle afforded by years of boat building successes. Some died young,

Arthur aboard the *Asia* and James died at 40 of paralysis. Jane went to New York and became a nurse. Hiram lived at home and worked in the boat yard. If any one of the children were born with the proverbial silver spoon in their mouths, it would have been Fred, the youngest. He had the experience and expertise of his father and older brothers to draw from. He became a consummate craftsman and athlete. He was arguably the best boat builder of the family.

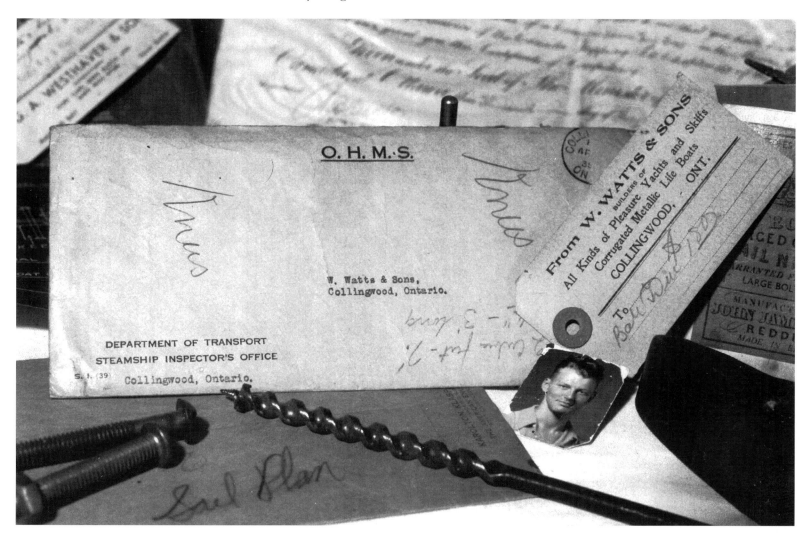

Referred to as a Collingwood 'Smacker', this was clearly a racing design. Part of the crew is seen sitting down in the hold. National Archives of Canada C13168

12 PLEASURE BOATS

FROM WORK TO PLAY

An integral part of human nature is competition. When the early hands of time began to move, the competition was brutal. The brutality of the contest was for a single purpose, survival.

People have progressed somewhat over the years, refining and channeling emotions down different avenues than those of our ancestors. Boats have a rich history of competition. From the very early craft that sailed, the need was always there to be bigger, faster, and carry more.

"The winning sailor, consistently does everything just a little bit better than the competition. He anticipates wind shifts more accurately than the rest...plays his sails with more finesse, handles his boat more effectively, knows his competition better, and has a sounder pro-active routine. Winning sail boat races is never magical nor mechanical. There are no shortcuts. It takes thoroughly practiced skills and a thoroughly practical philosophy." [1]

"believe me my young friend there is nothing, absolutely nothing, half so much worth doing as simply messing about in boats."

Kenneth Grahame,
1859–1932
Wind in the Willows

There are two kinds of yachts that exist. The first is the craft designed from the keel to the topmast for yachting. The second is the work boat, craft that have their design roots deep in practical applications.

A number of vessels built at the Watts yard were given all the necessary credentials needed for working. They could be fish boats, cargo carriers or passenger craft. One of the most famous of the Watts boats to make this transformation was the Collingwood fish boat.

The early skiffs of the lakes were virtually all constructed for the fishing industry. If not fishing, then carrying a variety of cargo was the role of the skiff in the 1800's. As the once–bountiful fishing industry began to dwindle, and when the great

1. Turner and Jobson. *The Racing Edge.* Simon and Schuster, 1979.

The "Silver Spray" Y. M. C. A. Camp Lake Couchiching.

The carrying capacity and the versatility of the Collingwood Skiff are clear in this image of the Silver Spray, *used by a Y.M.C.A. camp at Lake Couchiching, Ontario.* Watts Collection

catches fell off, many men in the business of fishing began to evaluate their once lucrative and colourful way of life.

A direct result of the decline of the fishing industry was the number of boats that became available at low prices. During this period there were literally hundreds of Collingwood fish boats either laid up, or put up for sale. The more unfortunate skiffs were left to rot or were cut up for firewood.

The decline of one industry usually has benefit to another. This was no exception. The boats were there, and the Collingwood fish boat would lend itself perfectly to the pursuit of pleasure boating. This would begin the first transformation of the proud fish boats that had become famous across Canada.

The skiff's changes and adaptations for yachting were minimal, considering the design purpose of a work boat. The most major change was not to the boat's design, but to her name. They were originally named Collingwood fish boats, identifying them with their birthplace and function. The vessels later became Collingwood Skiffs or Mackinaws. These names were added to give the boat a higher social status or allure than a fish boat. Captain William Watts recalls the early boats were "not called Mackinaws, but just Collingwood fish boats. The name mackinaw came much later, and it is just possible the Straits of Mackinac between Huron and Michigan may have something to do with it. Our Collingwood fishermen frequently went to Detour at the mouth of Sault Ste. Marie River and fished right up to the Straits before

there was any government restrictions on Lake Huron. I suppose it would be called 'boatlegging' today." [2]

The boat's broad acceptance as a successful design, and its subsequent use all over Canada may explain some of the regional name changes.

The skiffs were very fast and sea-worthy with their working rigging. The rigging set-ups that allowed the fisherman's speed and manoeuvrability were the same qualities a yachtsman would find of value.

"When fish boats become yachts, they tend to be given a more attractive name for public consumption. Mystic Seaport records that "Maine sloop boats of the lobster fishery became friendship sloops, named after one of the villages that built them. As Great Lakes fishermen turned to gas boats, some fish boats went yachting. Marine historian C. H. J. Snider wrote: "Yacht clubs began to use the term mackinaw, often shortened to Mac (Snider 42). Watts of Collingwood built a half dozen for the National Yacht Club of Toronto. But by the 1930's, few remained in yachting. Their shoal draft made them grand gunkholers, but most yachtsman preferred the standing head room and stability of an enclosed keel boat. The Watts fish boats also have been called Collingwood Skiffs. The Watts business letter-head listed some of the types of boats the shop built, including skiffs. But this meant something different. One such skiff for the Department of Marine and Fisheries was shipped to Port Credit so that light keeper John Miller could row out and tend

2. Captain William Watts Jr. to James Barry, September 1938.

Ken Jones, Nahma's *long time skipper.*
Collingwood Museum Collection

*Family of Sir Edmund Walker relaxing
aboard the* Nahma. From the files
of the late Dr. H.A.Hunter.

the crib lighthouse. She was a pretty 17-foot, clinker-built, sharp-sterned rowing skiff. Very different from the Collingwood fish boats that now have been termed skiffs. [3] ”

Nahma is one such boat that remains in existence as a testament to the work and yachting theories. She was the second such craft that was ordered from W. Watts & Sons by Sir Edmund Walker of Toronto, philanthropist and promoter of the Arts. He ordered his first skiff in 1890. *Nahma* would give countless hours of pleasure sailing on the waters of Lake Simcoe. The second *Nahma* was built in 1923, using the same standard rigging and iron work as her predecessor.

Nahma would go through a series of owners and eventually end up in the hands of Ken Jones. Ken Jones was a sailor and colourful fixture around Lake Ontario's yachting scene. Ken would keep *Nahma* alive and in competitive trim into the 1990's.

The Huron boat is another of the Watts-built craft to make the conversion to pleasure boating. Huron boats have been called the square-sterned version of the Collingwood Skiff. *Pequod* would be a typical example of the Huron design in yachting form. *Pequod* was built by the Watts firm c. 1920 registered at the prestigious Royal Canadian Yacht Club of Toronto. Although early records of her exploits are scant, *Pequod* was a fixture in the winner's circle at Port Credit yacht races until the 1970's. *Pequod* and *Nahma* were often entered in the same races. The Huron was much more yachtsman–friendly than her

stable mate, the Collingwood Skiff. The Huron-type design usually had a closed cabin with a fair amount of head room. The wide transom provided an area at the stern for an engine and seating of the crew.

Spanning the many years W. Watts & Sons constructed vessels from coast to coast, some truly remarkable craft were built. The working and yachting designs sometimes blur and run together. This is a blessing for both. While some may look down on the working craft, it should be noted, features from the working varieties are often implemented into pleasure versions which enhance their qualities. This trading of features has gone on as long as there have been boats and will continue for at least as long.

W. Watts & Sons would develop racing craft specifically for pleasure yachting and to showcase their designs throughout the Great Lakes area.

One such craft was the large, racy *Mocking Bird*. She was the crown jewel of Watts & Sons in the 1800's. Crewed by William Sr. and his sons, the *Mocking Bird* was noted for its incredible speed and winning record. *Mocking Bird* was loaded on flat cars and transported to different regattas by train. So proud of the yacht, the family had several oil paintings commissioned. Each member of her crew had one.

"Matthew was an ardent lover of sailing, and in his early years with his father toted the old *Mocking Bird* in ahead of all others on the Bay. And on one occasion, led those on Lake Simcoe to which the racer was transferred by rail." [4]

---

3. Joyce, Lorne. *Fish Boats in Sail,* Inland Seas, Spring 1997.

4. Enterprise-Bulletin. *Famed Boat Builder Has Passed Away,* June 17, 1935.

Nahma at Degrassi Point, Lake Simcoe, under the care of the Walker Family. From the files of the late Dr. H.A.Hunter.

Looking forward on Nahma's *standing rigging, 1985.*
Collingwood Museum Collection

Mocking Bird *was the Watts secret weapon in regattas all around the lakes. She's sporting different rigging here than she is in the facing page. The rig may have been altered from race to race to compete in different classes of sailing.* **Watts Collection**

Syren was another sleek craft to gain the Watts-built vessel accolades. *Syren* was designed and built on the West Coast by Captain William Watts Jr. She was also used as a showcase of the builder's designs and prowess. *Syren* was entered into the International Yacht race on the Pacific Coast July 4, 1891. From his youth in Collingwood, and his family record in regattas, Watts would take this competition very seriously. The results were a reflection of Watts as a designer, sailor and builder. A fine crew of six was assembled, with Watts at the helm.

Syren raced against seven American yachts and took the title. Of the boats defeated, two were keel boats, one a product of acclaimed U.S. designer Herreshoff. Ninety dollars in gold was presented to Watts, and was enjoyed by the crew at the local hotel. "I spent the $90 and more," chuckled Watts.

Captain Watts was a firm believer in the double-ended boat, with one concession. He did prefer the elliptical stern for pure yachting.

"There is no question that the pleasure yacht of the present day design is superior in some respects than your sharp stern fish boat can be. For instance your stern sheets, or sails, take up too much space on account of the narrow stern. The elliptic stern can be so designed to give you a good roomy cockpit, with floor up high enough to make it self-bailing."[5]

A number of other pleasure craft grew in reputation as W. Watts & Sons expanded. The sleek steam and fan tail launches made a valued and attractive contribution to the lakes. The launches were used commercially and for family endeavours, transferring guests to hotels and lodges on the early lakes. These rides were made enjoyable in the smooth riding, and sometimes extravagantly appointed launches. The launch could be simple or as opulent a design as the customer wanted. Some were merely used for picnics and excursions on the lakes and bays of the area. Launches were powered by a number of methods over the years. Steam, Naptha and gasoline were all popular at different times.

Mocking Bird *was the Watts family's own racing boat. She sailed in regattas near and far. This was taken in 1874. Even with wind in her sails* Mocking Bird *leaves no wake.* Collingwood Museum Collection

5. Captain William Watts Jr. to James Barry. April 25, 1939.

The Syren *was designed and built by the Watts & Trott boat yard in 1890.*
City of Vancouver Archives BO. P.152, N.152

Pequod is pictured here at the Port Credit Yacht Club. Her name comes from Herman Melville's novel Moby Dick.
Courtesy of Ken Maxwell

A charming steam launch escorts this family of four on an afternoon excursion. Collingwood Museum Collection

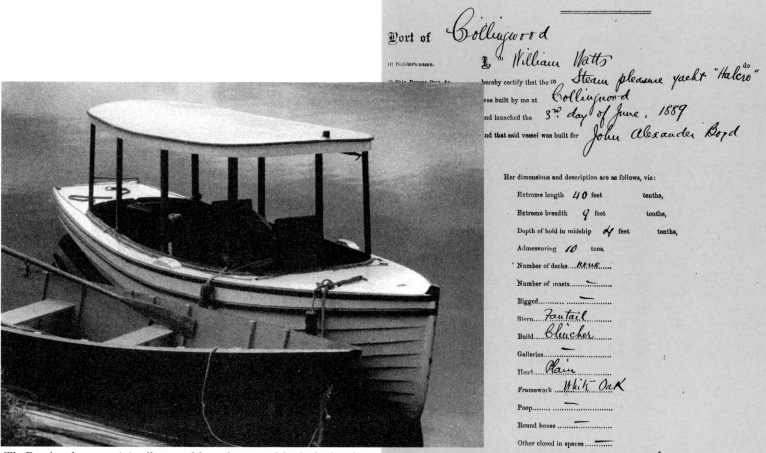

The Patriarch *was originally owned by a doctor in Meaford after the turn of the century. The 'Ark' as it was affectionately nicknamed still graces the Magnettewan River.* Marie Pearson Collection

Halcro *was a beautiful 40 ft. steam launch, built for the Boyd family of Georgian Bay.*

BUILDER'S CERTIFICATE

Under Merchant Shipping Act, 1854.

Port of Collingwood

(1) Builder's name. I, William Watts

hereby certify that the (2) Steam pleasure yacht "Halcro"
was built by me at Collingwood
and launched the 3rd day of June, 1889
and that said vessel was built for John Alexander Boyd

Her dimensions and description are as follows, viz:

Extreme length 40 feet tenths,

Extreme breadth 9 feet tenths,

Depth of hold in midship 4 feet tenths,

Admeasuring 10 tons.

Number of decks none

Number of masts

Rigged

Stern Fantail

Build Clincher

Galleries

Head Plain

Framework White Oak

Poop

Round house

Other closed in spaces

WITNESS my hand, this 12th
day of July 1889

SIGNED this 12th day of July, Wm. Watts
in the presence of

A. C. Reddell Witness.

Largo, *a pleasure yacht built for Harry Greening in the late 1930's. This is an unusual configuration with the cabin aft and centre cockpit.* Watts Collection

Largo in the spring of 1941 at Watts shop for alterations. Watts Collection

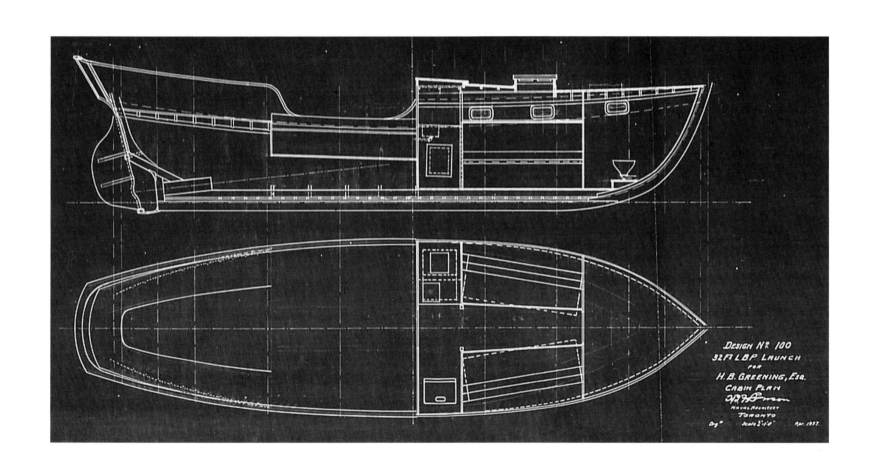

Cabin plan for Harry Greening's Largo.
Watts Collection

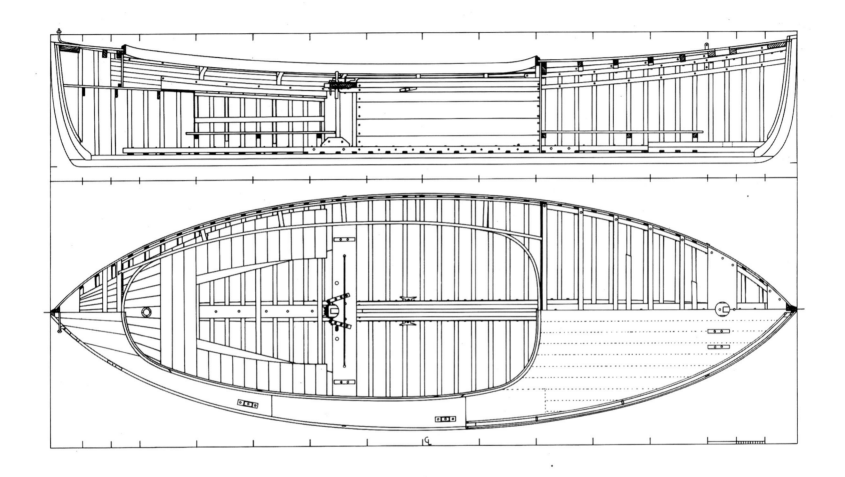

NAHMA

Nahma *lines and sail plan as detailed by Philip Gillese.* Courtesy of the
National Museum of Science and Technology, Ottawa, Canada.

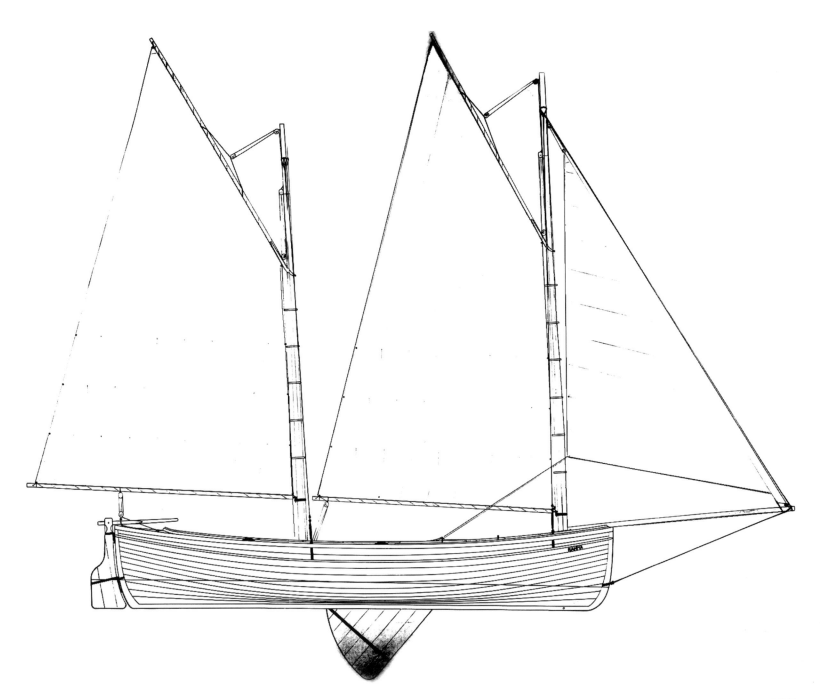

*Boats in tow on Georgian Bay 1914. Watts
and a number of other builders transported
boats from the shop to the customer in this fashion.*
Photo: Wm. James Topley,
National Archives of Canada PA 11198.

13 MOLDS, METHODS & MATERIALS

STEM TO STERN

"When I was a young boy the shop was a real meeting place, especially in the winter months, this is when all the old Captains and the guys on the lakes would come into the shop and sit around the stove, trade tales and watch the boats being built," recalled Reg Watts.

When entering a traditional boat building shop, you have the feeling of being taken back to a simpler time. The smell of freshly sawn cedar, the aroma of oakum, and the drone of the line shaft turning all the equipment, creates an all–encompassing experience. The traditional shop is about the five senses: sight, sound, touch, smell and the taste for the craft that carries many rich traditions. In fact, those fortunate enough to have been exposed to the experience can recall it at will many years later.

The shop of W. Watts & Sons was no different. Bustling with activity summer and winter, craftsmen went about their duties oblivious to all but their own tasks. To an outsider looking in, one is in awe at the array of skills, machinery, materials and half-finished hulls on the shop floor that somehow all fit together to form a finely-crafted vessel. The Watts yard was located with most of the raw materials needed in close proximity. This abundant supply enabled them to tap into virgin growth. White cedar, white oak, white ash–the Watts' materials of choice–were often hand-picked to suit their needs. Fred Hodgson, an early settler, recalls the majesty of the forest:

> "The lofty elm, the stately ash, the vigorous maple, the beau brummel
> beech, the dainty balsam, the fragrant cedar and the bride–decked birch,
> an occasional giant pine with its crown of emerald...fringes of low alba
> vitae, ran along the indentations of the lake front, with curling ivies
> and climbing vines clinging to their nut–brown branches." [1]

Man is preeminently a creative animal, predestined to strive consciously for an object and to engage in engineering – that is, incessantly and eternally to make new roads wherever they may lead.

Feodor Dostoevski,
1821–1881

---

1. Hodgson, Fred. 1894.

157

In the early days, the Watts boys did their own lumbering, out of necessity more than choice for the most part. The craftsman who really loved his work had no greater joy than to have the knowledge to select a tree that just suited the task. Matthew and William had the opportunity and the knowledge to choose the very best of the timber, which in turn was reflected in the finished product. To have this kind of quality control is a significant factor in the reputation for excellence built by W. Watts & Sons in the years to come.

As the business grew and time was of the essence, the local mills began to feed the shop's hungry appetite. This required a separate building just for storage of wood in varying stages of readiness. The storage shed was located to the west of the main building. It was about 28' at the peak and of post and beam construction, with a dirt floor. The material would be sawn and delivered with the bark still on it, these were known as flitches. The lumber would be sorted by variety, with grading of the lumber being done prior to it going into storage. As logging began to strip away a lot of the old growth forests, the choice timber for boat building went with it. As early as the late 1930's, the Watts company was buying up large numbers of log homes and barns to get the cedar timbers that were needed for planking.

The wooden boat builder–90% of the time–wanted straight grain lumber free of knots; the exception would be the crooks, cut from certain areas of the trees, roots included where the grain ran at sharp angles. The use of crook sawn lumber was for structural integrity. In the cutting of stems, knees and other components that required rigidity, if the curve of the wood was right, steaming and severe bending could be minimized. The woods used by Wm. Watts & Sons were white cedar, white oak and ash. Maple was used in limited quantities, with more exotic woods such as cypress, mahogany, and teak being more of a customer preference.

At W. Watts & Sons, the mold loft was located on the second floor of the main shop. The main shop was 80 to 90 feet long, with heavy wooden floors, the exterior walls covered in board and batten. Windows were large and numerous. In the mold loft, the windows were positioned close to the floor to assist in keeping a bright work area. The mold loft also doubled as the sail makers loft. Both these jobs required large expanses of uncluttered floor space. Most of the boats would be constructed off full size molds made in the loft. Sail making and drawing out the boats shapes on the loft floor is a very specialized part of the boat building. In the early years most shops completed these tasks on their own.

Half models were made from the blue print. The size of the half model was in direct relation with the scale of the blue print. The old craftsmen would carve a half model of the boat, which had to be extremely accurate. The reason for this accuracy was that any design flaws that could not be seen in the drawing, would likely be noticed in the half model. The half model gave the designer or builder a three–dimensional look at a one-dimensional drawing. The half model is the link between the concept on paper and a completed boat. Some may see the half model today as more of a decorative piece, but it was an important tool in the architecture and construction of any boat. Through the half model, the shape of the hull could be seen, studied and corrected before molds, and the actual craft was built. Wm. Watts & Sons usually built their half models in the lift style, constructed of horizontal slats. They were typically constructed of a soft wood, bass wood, pine or cedar. "The old fella just sat down and whittled them out," said Reg Watts about his grandfather.

The Watts shop employed the services of Matthew

Matthew Walton, sailmaker for W. Watts & Sons.
John Walton Collection

Walton as sail maker. Reg Watts recalls, "They used to say that old William could really churn out the sail work in those days, it was all sewn by hand." A limited variety of sail materials were available at that time. The Watts shop used canvas, cotton, linen and silk on special orders. Canvas was a versatile material around the shop. Apart from sails, most builders used canvas as deck covering, a covering for sea anchors, canopies and curtains for many of the early craft. molds were built in the mold loft, hence the name. Often, the only clear floor space available was the loft or upper area of the shop. The blueprints were taken upstairs, and full–size shapes were drawn on the floor from the blueprints. Rough cut lumber, usually 1" boards of pine, were cut out and nailed together to form the molds that were erected down in the shop. These molds were beveled on the edge, so the planks would lie over them to give the boat its shape. They were a removable skeleton. The job in the mold loft of laying down the boat lines on the loft floor and constructing and shaping the molds off these lines required extreme attention to detail.

William Watts was a tradesman who built by eye, a skill that was rare then and has virtually disappeared today. Recalling this methods, William Watts Jr. notes:

"We were the only people building these boats without molds to keep them in shape. We planked them right up to the sheer strake then bent the steamed frames into place as well as the floors and kept them in shape by shoring outside. I think I must have mentioned that my father learned the business in Ireland, where he built all clinker boats for sailing ships..."[2]

The main building was set up to take the wood in at one end, do all the milling and fitting, then move the timber out to the construction area for finish and assembly. The front part of the shop was where the machinery was positioned. This equipment had to be able to handle the

A boat takes shape inside the W. Watts & Sons shop. Boats were constructed right side up, this one with only 4 molds. Cleve Walton is standing far right, the man in the centre is Henderson, a neighbour to Watts on Maple Street. Collingwood Museum Collection

daily rigours of boat building as well as the sometimes huge sizes of wood that would come in to the shop. Initially run by steam to a line shaft, before being operated by electricity. The equipment was all positioned to best utilize the limited floor space. A 36" marine band saw was used in the Watts shop. This type of band saw differs

from a regular band saw in that the entire unit rotates around the table. The table stayed flat so the men would not have to move the large timbers needed for boat building. Other standard equipment used in the Watts shop was the shaper, the planer, drill presses, assorted band saws, a large and small table saw, a jointer and a multitude of related hand tools.

Once the materials were in the construction area, the finishing touches were put on planks, stems and keels prior to final assembly. The walls of the assembly area were lined with dozens of hand planes, chisels, and clamping equipment. The large steam box was located along the east wall. Steam was provided by a large cast iron vertical tube boiler. The construction method Watts employed was that all their craft were built right side up. Smaller boats were laid down on a strong back and the larger boats had the keel laid on the floor. A level wooden floor is essential for a commercial boat building operation. The floor becomes an integral part of the boat, until such a stage as the boat is far enough along to support its own members.

The large spars and masts were selected from tall straight trees. The round logs would come in to the shop and were cut square to the approximate size needed. The four corners were then removed with a draw knife or adze depending on the size of the mast. This would leave 8 corners giving an octagonal shape to the timber. The process was continued until a round log was formed to size. The log was then finished with special planes and spoke shaves to give the mast its smooth, round shape.

The Watts shop was a self-sufficient unit. In its early days everything was made on the premises. This continued until the early 1920's, when the job of blacksmithing was farmed out to the local blacksmith shops. The main providers of this service were Deys of Collingwood. When Reg Watts was a kid helping out at the shop, he recalls:

"They built the whole works other than the blacksmithing. They always used different ones, whichever one was closest. I can hear him, "Reggie, come here, take this to the blacksmith shop." So, I'd take it to the closest one. In the earlier days, they even used the shop for cold storage, they used to store apples, vegetables, deer meat and fish for the winter." [3]

A variety of tradesmen were employed at the Watts shop: sail maker, tinsmith and shipwrights. Some of the men, such as the Waltons, were long- term employees. Others were seasonal, being employed mostly in the winter months. Reg Watts recalls:

"At one time, all eleven of the boys worked there, and my Aunt Daisy did the bookkeeping. One of the brothers was crippled in some way, but he was employed there as well. He would do the sawing, oar making and anything else he was able to do. A special chair was built on rollers and one arm of the chair was modified to make a holder for different tools. All he done was saw wood. They would shape a plank, and he'd cut it in two. He could really rip through those planks." [4]

When a boat is planked and frames are bent into place, only half the job is done. The next step is the fitting out. This was a time-consuming process, where in a lot of cases the builder really got to showcase his skills as a wood worker. Seats, knees, floor boards–all had to cut and fit into place. The cabin and interiors would have to be built, if the design required it. Spars had to be varnished and and the interior and exterior of the vessels painted. In a letter to James Barry, Capt. William Watts recalls:

"Painting you might say from the beginning was all done with white lead and oil, with a little turps to dry it and a little lamp black to colour it grey for inside or deck. Then later on we discovered yellow ochre for a cheaper paint and used it inside and on deck. I have seen tar used occasionally but never on a new boat, some poor chap that did not have the price. Occasionally some chap would put on an extra stripe or two similar to the ladies of today". [5]

Bud Akitt, who worked at the Collingwood shop as a youth, remembers how strong the paint was when hulls were being painted. "It'd smell for days," [6] Bud said. He recalls there being two different mixtures for the interior and exterior of the boats. White lead was the staple, with boiled oil for the interior and raw oil for the exterior.

A number of vessels were built off site. One such vessel was the *Mary S. Gordon*, a 56' schooner built on the shores of Kincardine in 1882. The keel was laid out-

3. Watts, Reg interviewed by Barbara Arp, May 1983.

4. Watts, Reg interviewed by Barbara Arp, May 1983
5. Captain William Watts Jr. to James Barry, November 1937.
6. Bud Akitt, in an interview with the authors, June 10, 1977.

Real horse power was used to haul boats out of the shop. In the photo, Fred Watts can be seen at the far left in the dark hat, overseeing the operation. After it comes out of the shop, the horses head for the water to launch. Photo: Ernie Brock, Watts Collection

W. WATTS & SONS BOAT BUILDERS

side in a clearing by the shore or any clear piece of land close to water.

When the boats were completed they were launched into the water right out the north doors or in to a slipway dug between the two main shops. The large craft would be hauled out of the shop in a cradle by block and tackle. The floors would be greased to cut down the friction. When larger boats reached the doors, a horse or team of horses would hook on and pull the boat out of the shop and into the water. If the boats were to be shipped by rail, they would be skidded to the rail spur and pulled onto the flat cars with tackles, then secured to the rail car.

While some techniques are common to a great number of boat builders, other techniques and methods are very particular to an individual craftsman. "There was much to learn and an interested man could gain a Ph.D's worth

of knowledge and experience. These yards no longer exist, nor does the knowledge."[7] It is often said, and in reality it happens, that a veteran boat builder will not give up his secrets of the trade. In some cases, upon their death, the craftsmen will have all their records destroyed. These are cases in the extreme. Boat building was, and is, a competitive and relatively small field of endeavour, where techniques might not be widely discussed. The fact is, a boat builder's knowledge is what makes him his living. More often than not, the great majority of these craftsman are more than forthcoming and helpful in providing information to those who are truly interested in the craft. It has been said by an old–time boat builder, "I don't tell just anybody how it's done, just those I think are worthy."[8]

As we think of builders of wooden boats, the obvious assumption might be made they are all masters of carpentry. In fact, time and time again the boat builder says, "I can't cut a 90–degree angle or saw a straight line." Rather than be a master of corners and squares, the boat builder is a master of a smooth curve or a rolling bevel.

Transporting boats by rail car was common place. This is Fred Watts' Navaid. Watts Collection

7. Thoms, Barry. *Building the Herreshoff Dinghy.* Mystic Seaport Museum, 1977
8. Ibid.

Spectators crouch at the stern of one of Fred Watts' last boats, watching the side launch of Murray Bay *at the Collingwood Shipyard, Spring 1960. Watts Collection.*

14 THE END OF THE COMPANY

BUT THE END IS NOT YET

Let your boat of life

be light, packed with only

what you need—a homely home

and simple pleasures, one or

two friends, worth the name,

someone to love and someone

to love you, a cat, a dog,

and a pipe or two, enough to

eat and enough to wear,

and a little more than

enough to drink; for

thirst is a dangerous thing.

Jerome Klapka Jerome,
1859–1927
Three Men in a Boat

Circumstance is a peculiar thing. A business that has a solid foundation in experience and production, like W. Watts & Sons, can usually survive one or even two significant setbacks. During the Depression and the early years of WWII, there were simply too many strikes against the boat–building business for it to survive. Some of the occurrences were entirely unavoidable. It was a specific time and place, and the people in the key roles had reasons for making the decisions they did. Those reasons made sense at the time. Fifty years later, it's easy to look back and think of solutions. Chances are, we'd all make different decisions if we could see the impact of them half a century later.

After the death of Matthew Watts, the only boat builder left to actually carry on production was 57-year-old Fred Watts, the youngest of William & Susan's children. Fred, nicknamed "Mossy", was a skilled craftsman and sailor like his brothers or father. He was widowed with two grown sons. Bill was 20, and Reg was 18. It was now up to this group of three to carry on a business that had over 80 years of history on the southern shores of Georgian Bay.

Bill and Reg, like so many Watts boys before them, were welcome and encouraged to work in the family business. They were both exposed to the operation long before their uncle Matthew's death and played different roles. As young boys they were often stuck with menial errands. Bill spent a lot of time on the waterfront, whether it was in the boat house or on the dock. Both boys were particularly athletic. Reg took to rowing. Other young men in Collingwood harbour seemed to enjoy diving off incredibly high platforms. They dove off the sheer legs, which was a tall, tripod-like crane used by the Collingwood Shipyard. If that wasn't high enough, they'd try the cabin of a freighter docked at the Grain Elevators. Bill Watts was noted for his diving. Many felt he was destined for Olympic competition.

Frederick Charles Watts and his wife Jean Wood.
Watts Collection

With so many government contracts, life boats and repairs, work at the boat shop was always available. The opportunity to work was there, but it didn't pay well. The wages for workers outside the family were different than those offered to Bill and Reg. For some reason, Fred chose to under pay his own sons. The labour they were subject to was as heavy, and at times, dirtier work than others were exposed to.

As a boy, Reg Watts earned $9 per week, and paid $7 in room and board. The ten cents per package of tobacco to roll his own cigarettes cut into the remaining profits. Ernie Brock, who worked under Fred when both sons were helping build boats, was paid 35¢ an hour, while Bill Watts was being paid 25¢. "It drove Bill nuts," Brock recalls.

Art Drever, a Collingwood commercial fisherman, recalls an incident with his family's fish tug, the *Leighton McCarthy*. After a day's work near Midland, they headed for Collingwood. Without any notice, the pin fell from the rudder, and left them without any navigational control to land safely in the harbour. Without the advent of radar, the only guide they had for Collingwood was the sound of the rivetters working against the

steel hulls in the Shipyard. After school on a frosty November afternoon, Bill and Reg Watts put the rudder pin back in while *Leighton McCarthy* was still in the water. With their school clothes on, they dove into the frigid waters to put the rudder back in place. "I'll never forget that," Drever said.

Both sons would have been more than pleased to take over the family operation, as Fred had before them, and their uncle Matthew before. For whatever reasons, both felt isolated from the heart of the operation. They were given jobs to do, but not enough. Reg Watts later said he would have settled for less money, but he was never given

Two Collingwood fish tugs at the wharf. Annie M *sports a W. Watts & Sons built life boat.* Leighton McCarthy *was operated by the Drever family.* John Boyd Collection, National Archives of Canada PA 71649

Bill (left) and Reg Watts sitting on the porch of their Pine Street home, Collingwood. Watts Collection

the time and training to feel comfortable building the boats. Time was spent with other young men, but not Reg and Bill.

The inequities of the operation sent both boys looking for employment elsewhere.

Bill, the oldest, chose the path of many Collingwood men before him. Bill went sailing. Sailing on the lake freighters would put more money in the bank than working for Dad at 25¢ an hour. He joined the crew aboard *Portwell*, a 259-foot canal-sized bulk freighter built for Scott Misener Steamships Limited. Bill would have been familiar with this kind of vessel in Collingwood harbour. It was the kind that he and his buddies would use as a diving platform.

In 1938, while the *Portwell* was near Valleyfield, Quebec, Bill Watts took his last dive off the hull. He hit a rock and sustained serious head injuries. Reg boarded the first train he could to see him in a Quebec hospital. He died shortly after. Reg returned home to Collingwood, with the body of his brother on the train. Bill Watts was 23.

The ordeal was almost more than Reg could bear. He never talked much about his brother to people outside the family. When asked about the boat building business, Reg would always say "My brother was the boat builder." Bill was two years older, and by rights had more experience than his younger brother, but Reg would reveal years later that he too learned a few things in his early days inside the Watts Boat shop.

Reg left his Father's employ in 1937 for The Collingwood Shipyards. The Yard wasn't as busy as it had been. During the 30's, only three vessels were built, a hydrographic steamer in 1931, a minesweeper for the Defense Department in 1938, and a tanker for Imperial Oil also in 1938. There were refits, repair work and even some non-traditional work. In an effort to keep the workers employed, Shipyard management sought and won contracts to manufacture cement mixers, metal castings, sand hoppers and oil tanks. Regardless of the product, Reg had work that paid. At that time, wages at the Yard ranged between 40¢ and 58¢ an hour. Even at the lowest end of the scale, he would have brought home nearly double what Fred felt was an appropriate weekly salary for his sons.

1946

Price List

Johnson Sea Horse Outboard Motors

Model
HD 2.5 h.p. With Ready-Pull
    Starter $125.00
TD 5 h.p. With Ready-Pull
    Starter 170.00
KD 9.8 N.O.A. Certified Brake
    Horse Power with Ready-
    Pull Starter 250.00
    KDL available with 6" longer
    driveshaft, $8.00 extra.
OK 8.1 N.O.A. Certified Brake
    Horse Power 215.00
    OKL available with 5" longer
    driveshaft, $8.00 extra.
SD 16 N.O.A. Certified Brake
    Horse Power, Streamlined
    Powerhead, with Ready-
    Pull Starter 335.00
PO 22 N.O.A. Certified Brake
    Horse Power 370.00
    Models SDL and POL avail-
    able with 6" longer driveshaft
    $16.00 extra.

All prices are subject to change without notice, and are f.o.b. factory, Peterboro, 8% Sales Tax included.

Johnson Motors
PETERBORO   CANADA
10M P.P.Co. 46-456

For a time Fred Watts had the Johnson Motor dealership in Collingwood. It was later sold to Tom Smalley. Watts Collection

By the late 1930's, Fred was the only Watts in the boat house. He had a crew of workers, and by all reports, plenty of work to be done. Lighthouse tenders came in for regular repair, life boats, and government contracts. The Depression never had an impact on their operation. Young men in Collingwood would have given their eye teeth to work with Fred Watts. One such man was an inquisitive and fiery youth known as 'Steamer' Clark. He approached Fred to give him work in the boat shop without pay. 'Steamer' wanted to learn to do what Fred did, create a fine boat skillfully and expertly. He had built his own boat at the age of 17, and knew he wanted to do it again. Fred flat-out denied him the opportunity to work with him. 'Steamer' still remembers this incident decades later. "Why a guy wouldn't hire a fella to work for nothing...I offered to go down there and just learn how to build."

All the work didn't happen in the shop. Fred Watts and employees
Cleve Walton and Tom Hyatt pass the time away near the launch slip.
Watts Collection

'Steamer's' ambition would have been a red flag for Fred Watts. Others have thought that whatever Watts secret was, it was guarded. Perhaps Fred thought if someone else knew what made the boat shop tick, he'd have to compete. The truth of the matter was that Watts' boats were being imitated all over, and their influences were seen across the nation. 'Steamer' went on to build a few more boats, without Fred's instruction.

Another young man approached Fred with the same offer, free labour for an education in boat building. This time around, Fred took on 'Bud' Akitt. He was only 17 or 18 and had never stepped foot inside a high school. "It was just teaching, learning. Better than on the street," Bud recalls. In his time at the boat shop, during the late 30's, Bud saw the repair of life boats and lighthouse tenders. He still marvels at Fred's aptitude in the shop. "I've seen him cut wood...he could have a pencil mark in along–and he'd just walk along a 16 or 18 foot plank and just....Watts! You know, he was used to it...He was a good man to be around...well, if he could get any work out of you all right, but you'd learn. It was training. That's all it was. It was really training."

'Bud' Akitt found favour with Fred Watts. "I got along good with him, I don't know why," he said. "We often talked, he explained things. I was the only one in there interested in learning anything. He was always good."

As the 1940's approached, Fred's health declined. A government contract for 21 new boats was awarded to the firm of W. Watts & Sons. Fred Watts, once able to handle himself in almost any situation, was no longer able to build boats. He was at the beginning of a long and painful battle with cancer.

He only had two employees in the boat house, Ernie Brock and Cleve Walton. The Waltons had worked for

CHEQUES ISSUED						
DATE	No.	To Whom Payable		Deposits	Amount of Cheque	Balance
April 18		Albert Parrish			105 00	
May		Albert Parrish			100 00	
July 15		F. Lewis			200 00	
July 30		London Life			27 04	
march 20		F. G. Watts			205 00	

One of the very few records showing salaries at the Boat Shop. This was from the early 1940's. Fred Watts and Albert Parrish are the only two noted here. Watts Collection

Fred for quite some time, and built a few boats in their own back yard. For one reason or another Fred didn't give Cleve the option of taking on the 21 boats.

His son Reg was settled into a promising career at the Collingwood Shipyard. The Yard paid well and Fred didn't, if he paid at all.

Fred's first choice for someone to take on these 21 boats should have been Reg, but it was too late for both of them. By now, Fred recognized his failure to invest in the future by teaching his sons more of the business and the craft. He always had time for just about everybody, but not his own family. Reg had made his own way without his father, and would continue along that path.

The only option Fred Watts had to keep the business going was Ernie Brock. Brock was no amateur himself. He singlehandedly constructed a fine 24-foot motor launch named for his wife, Joan. *Joan* was later sold to the Shipyard. Fred made frequent trips to Ernie's shop to investigate his construction methods.

One visit was more than a social call. "I want you to take on these 21 boats," Fred said. "I'll give you the shop. I can't work, but I'll be there to help you out." Ernie Brock told Fred he didn't have the skills to do it. "You built this boat without anybody else around," prompted Fred. Brock declined the offer.

With few options left, Fred took his contract for 21 boats and offered it to Cliff Richardson of Meaford. Richardson built a few boats in his back yard. He was a frequent visitor to Fred's shop in Collingwood, looking for pointers and a lesson or two from Watts. During the summers he and his father operated A.H. Richardson's Boat Garage at Pike Bay in Pointe au Baril. The Pike Bay operation was strictly repair, no boat building. The Boat Garage was established around 1914. The odd boat was built in Meaford, but no real production to speak of until 1939.

The order for 21 boats was accepted by Richardson, and he built a boat works on Meaford's waterfront, which is still in operation. Twenty-one boats, a government contract and Fred Watts to help out along the way. How could he resist such an offer? It was the offer that put Richardson's into boat production in earnest. "I remember at one time a blueprint of a life boat around here with the Watts name on it," recalls Alan Richardson, Grandson of the founder. "At that time, all these drawings had to be certified. Once the government certified a drawing, if they gave you an order, you had to build to that drawing. That would have to be in the late '30's or early '40's," he added. He also recalls trips to Collingwood when his father would meet with Fred Watts in the boat house. As far as Alan can recall now, the meetings were to discuss the drawings of the government life boats.

The door was opening for Richardson's, and closing for Watts. Fred did repairs for local boaters, fishermen and more government tenders. W. Watts and Sons would not see the kind of production that once occurred.

The Second World War brought unprecedented work to the Collingwood Shipyard. Corvettes were ordered from many Canadian Yards. Collingwood was no different. The race was on to see who could launch the first Corvette. The war also called Reg Watts to join the Navy. In 1942 he left Collingwood for service on the Atlantic and Pacific coast, leaving his young wife and infant son Bill in the care of friends and family at home.

The Collingwood Shipyard was in the game. They had expertise, experience and a huge community effort to support them. They needed more space to lay out the Corvette plans and create a shipwright shop. Watts boat shop was in a prime spot. It was in close proximity to the Shipyard buildings, in fact, could easily have been mistaken for one if not for the sign identifying it to be otherwise. The size was perfect, already laid out with tools and equipment and an upper loft.

Interior of Richardson's Boat Works on Meaford Harbour.
Alan Richardson Collection

Reg Watts with his wife Willa and son Bill. During WW2 Reg served in Halifax and Vancouver. Watts Collection

W. WATTS & SONS BOAT BUILDERS

In support of the war effort, Fred was asked to sell his boat yard to the Shipyard. His health was steadily declining and there were no family members who could take over the business. The Watts shop was sold, with most of the equipment in it, so Collingwood could build Corvettes.

In a draft letter to the Department of Transport, Fred Watts writes:

Gentlemen;

The property of W. Watts & Sons and buildings have been sold to The Collingwood Shipyards (Yards) Ltd. as they required the space for the building of Corvettes. I sold it to them. Machinery, building and property. I have moved to another building we had as a stor (sic) house and intend carrying on the business as usual under the same name of William Watts & Sons. And in order to carry on, I would like to purchase a small ban (sic) saw and small surface playner (sic). I have been in Toronto for a few days and saw just what I want in Akinhead's Hardware and can get same as soon as you give me permission to buy same. I have work for a fishing company at Port Dover. The Colby Fish Co. And as soon as I get your permission to by machinery I can get more work. the band saw costs $180.00. the Playner (sic) will cost $90.00. Hoping you can do something for me as soon as possible, so I can get my order in to Aikenhead's before they sell those machines. If they sell them, I will be two months before they can fill my order.

He had noted that he "expected more work" initially, and then changed the letter to reflect that work would only be forthcoming if the equipment was in place. After almost 90 years in business in Collingwood, the Watts boat shop could always expect more work, equipment or not.

The sale price of the boat yard, property and equipment is unknown. Fred did get the new equipment he requested. Watts was a clever negotiator. He managed to acquire more than just money and new band saws in the deal struck with the Shipyard. The Collingwood Shipyard agreed that any member of the Watts family would have gainful employment at the Shipyard if they wanted it, as long as the Yard was in operation. They were also given access to the waterfront through yard property when it was needed for boat launches. Any specialized equipment that the Shipyard had, that may be required in boat construction, had to be shared.

W. Watts & Sons shop was now the Collingwood Shipyard's Shipwright's Shop. Its walls, floors and loft would never see the construction of wooden craft again, but preparation for the construction of Canada's first commissioned corvette, *H.M.C.S. Collingwood*. Fred moved into the life boat storage building and continued.

Navaid was one of the last of a number of vessels to be turned out of by Fred. She was a 36-foot, carvel, transom stern boat. *Navaid* became Fred's personal boat. In the 1950's it was sold to the Department of Transport for $3,970 and used as a lighthouse and buoy service boat. The Grey Marine gas engine of 111 b.h.p. was sold with it. In 1968 it was brought forth to Crown Assets for disposal. Throughout the 1970's, *Navaid* had multiple owners around Sorel and Montreal, Quebec. By 1976, the classification for

THE Callander

• BRASS
• GREY IRON
• BRONZE AND
• ALUMINUM CASTINGS

• S. & S. ELECTRICAL FITTINGS
• BEAVER POWER TOOLS

FOUNDRY & MFG. CO. LIMITED

73 MARKET ST. TORONTO
GUELPH, ONTARIO

SOLD TO W. Watts & Sons,
Collingwood, Ont.

DATE April 30/46

INVOICE NO. 2322

SHIPPED TO same

ROUTE Direct Winters   TERMS 1/10/n/30
D.S. 2977 Apr. 30

S.T.Lic.14

71102 0

ORDER NO.	BDLS	BAGS	DESCRIPTION	NET WEIGHT	PRICE	
Letter 4/29		36 pair	Fig. #297 2¼" Round Rowlocks, consisting of: 72 Rowlocks 72 Sockets		.88 pair	$ 31.68

Rec'd Payment May 7/46

The Callander Foundry & Manufacturing Co. Limited

E.R.Gordon

*Despite the advanced stages of cancer, Fred was still bringing in supplies in
1946. This was however, the end of his labours as a boat builder.*
Watts Collection

Nova Scotia Oar & Block Works Ltd.
SUCCESSORS TO

G. A. WESTHAVER & SON

MANUFACTURERS OF

BOAT OARS, SHIPS' BLOCKS, LUMBER

MAHONE BAY, N.S. June 17, 1946.

W. Watts & Sons,
Collingwood, Ontario.

Dear Sirs:

Since receipt of your letter of May 29th, we have made you a
shipment of oars and have been endeavouring to find a source of supply
for a carload of shingles.

Shingles are evidently scarce and are in big demand. I have
located 2 suppliers who are as yet undecided whether or not they would
be interested in each supplying a half carload to make a full carload
shipment. It seems that all of these shingle mills are able to sell
their shingles right at the mills, the buyers taking delivery in their
own trucks, and, we suspect, some cases paying above the retail ceiling
price.

No. 1 pine is almost impossible to get, although they might
supply a few in the carload. These people will not sell below the
retail ceiling price, which is as follows:

	Spruce	Pine	Hemlock
No. 1	$7.15	$7.45	$6.85
No. 2	5.95	6.25	5.65

If they can be induced to supply them at all, the car would
be largely composed of No. 2 and would be assorted.

Sincerely yours,

(A. Earle Giffin)
Managing Director.

AEG/ABM

*Clearly, despite his illness, Fred was still approaching every day
with ambition and productivity. This letter shows a shipment of
oars was sent in the summer of 1946.* Watts Collection

Navaid was changed from a lighthouse and buoy service boat to a yacht.

At the conclusion of the war, Reg came home and settled back into the Rigger's department at the Shipyard. He was well on his way to a supervisory position. His preference was the boat house, but it was too late. Fred was too frail and sick to do anything but feel remorse at the pending loss of his family's traditions. He knew his son was not properly equipped to simply carry on the business without interruption like he had. After a long battle with cancer, Frederick Charles Watts died in June of 1947.

The life boat storage house now stood empty. By all reports of those who knew him, Fred would not have entertained retirement. He was 69 when he died, and was as active as he was able to be in the last few years of his life. Production of the much–sought–after Watts boats ground to a halt in the post-war period.

There would be no more gatherings around the old stove in the boat house, telling stories, throwing another stick in the fire and watching Fred drink pint after pint of milk. A few row boats and Fred's 36–foot *Navaid* were reminders of a magnificent chapter in Canadian small craft history.

The close of the Watts boat building company didn't deter a few government departments from continuing to send tender documents to the family. Well over a decade beyond Fred's death, invitations to submit quotations for new boats were common place, even though they weren't replied to.

Reg Watts would stay in the Rigger's department and

lived less than a block from the life boat storage house that he maintained ownership of. His three sons would grow up with the boat house as a backdrop to their daily lives, a private and intriguing playground. The lure of his family's heritage, combined with his experience in steel shipbuilding, sparked Reg to bring boat building back to the boat house. This time, it was a project for private use. The days of commercial boat building by W. Watts & Sons were over after a century on the Great Lakes.

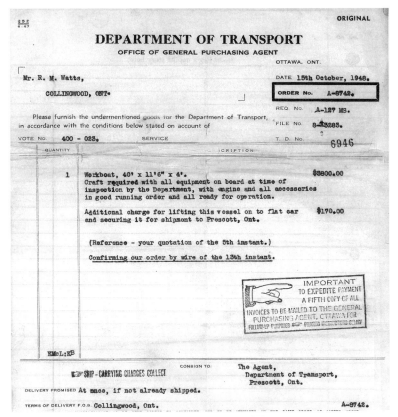

Bill of sale of the Navaid *to the Department of Transport.*
Watts Collection

The Navaid *used by the Department of the Marine in Prescott.* Watts Collection

Naviaid *taking the rails from Collingwood to Prescott. This photo was taken behind the Collingwood Railway Station.* Watts Collection

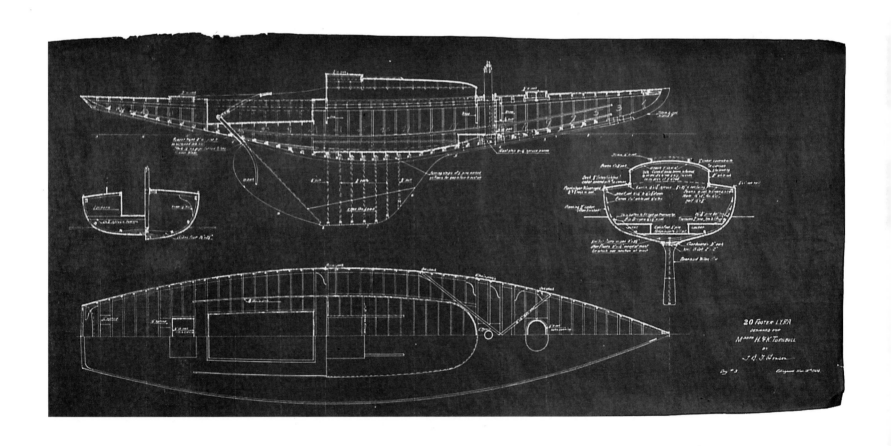

This sailboat can be seen leaving the Watts shop on Page 162.
Watts Collection

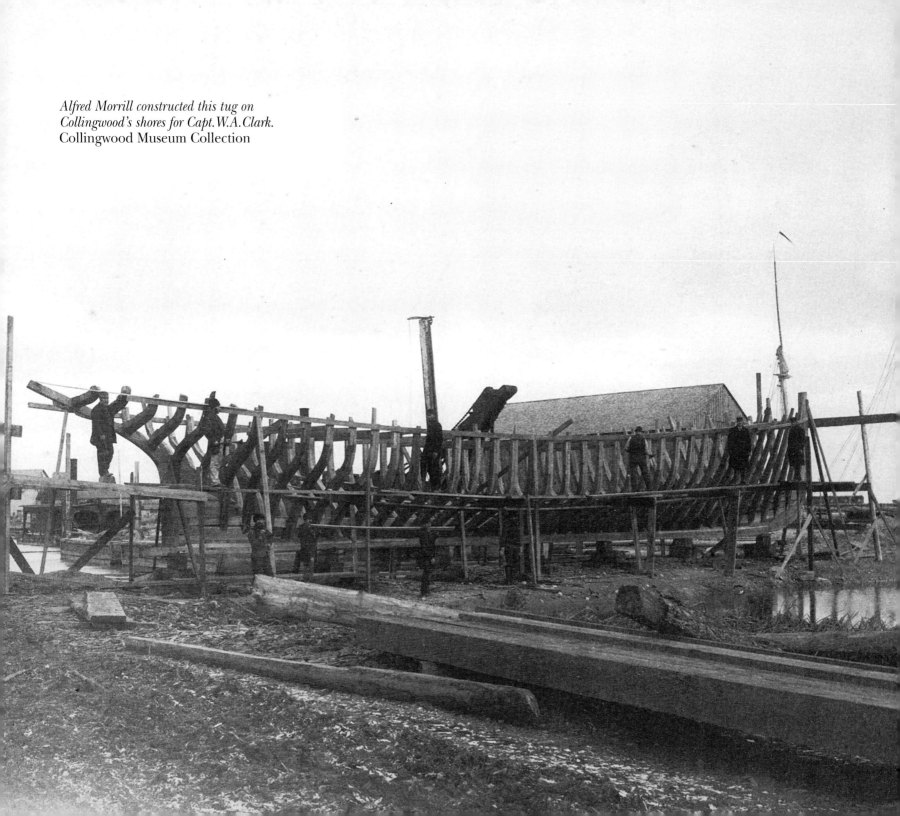

*Alfred Morrill constructed this tug on
Collingwood's shores for Capt. W.A. Clark.*
Collingwood Museum Collection

15 IMITATION IS THE FINEST FORM OF FLATTERY INFLUENCE OF WATTS DESIGN

Thou shalt not covet,

but tradition approves

all forms of competition.

Arthur Hugh Clough,
1819–1861
The Latest Decalogue

If imitation is the best form of flattery, then William Watts and his sons can consider many boat builders that followed their example to have paid them a huge compliment. Watts was largely influenced by the wooden boats being built in Ireland prior to his emigration. The family oral tradition points to William working as a boat builder before he came to Canada, and likely during his short return to the Emerald Isle when he married Susan Newton.

Watts was one of the pioneer boat builders of the new Dominion. With his first craft being constructed on Toronto Island prior to 1850, he was in a position to influence others because he was an existing builder. He was there, but he was also good, evidenced by the longevity of the company, and the sheer number of craft built by him around the lakes. There were more fish boats on the lakes in the last half of the 19th century than any other craft. They were so commonplace, the need to document their origins and their influences was likely seen as unnecessary.

The Watts influence can be seen wherever they built boats, and where they sailed. In Collingwood, Alfred Morrill set up his boat building shop about 1869, almost two decades after the establishment of Watts. Morrill was born in Nottingham England, and immigrated to Canada with his parents in 1844. They settled at Streetsville, where Alfred took up the trade of wagon making. While still in the region, he worked as a shipbuilder in Oakville before coming to Collingwood at 39.

The mainstay of Morrill's business were larger wooden tugs and work boats. The *Fred Hotchkiss* was a lumber carrier, reputed to be able to carry a million feet of lumber at one time. Three years later he built the *Louie Hotchkiss*, it was reported to be the largest wooden boat built on Collingwood's shores at that time. Morrill never actually owned any waterfront property, but conducted business along the site of the Collingwood Shipyard Dry Dock No. 2. He is credited with an

Salmon gillnet fleet at Steveston, Fraser River, B.C. William Watts Jr. built hundreds of boats for the Pacific fishing trade. National Archives of Canada. PA59998

A fleet of fish boats on the shore of Gimli, Manitoba. Collingwood fishermen ventured to Manitoba after the fish stocks in Lake Superior declined. National Archives of Canada. PA44894

impressive list of vessels, largely barges and tugs. Because of their size, many of his boats were constructed on the shores where they were ordered. The *Cisco* (1918), *Gordon Brown* (1901) and *Verda Belle* (1908) were all built at Port Stanley. *L'Marchieheal Foch* was built for Joseph Roque at Killarney in 1923, and *Frank G. Macaulay* was built at Southampton in 1898.

When it came to pleasure yachts, there is no mistaking where Morrill was influenced. The *Maggie A*, a pleasure yacht constructed for lumber and shipping businessman James Playfair, clearly has a heritage which stems back to the Watts boat yard. Even the black-painted hull echoes the untraditional black hull of Watts favourite racing yacht *Mocking Bird*.

Patrick Doherty also constructed a few boats, similar to the Collingwood Skiff, but not on as grand a scale as Watts. Doherty and Watts were both involved in the Masonic Lodge. Doherty started his boat building career as one of Watts many apprentices. There would have been many marine discussions in the Manito Lodge about who built the better boat. Doherty later turned to brick-laying.

Ike Van Koughnet, another Collingwood man, built a few boats for personal and commercial use. He also started his career in the Watts boat shop.

In Midland, Gidley's boat works was established around 1882. According to Captain Watts of Vancouver, Gidley worked for him at his yard on the Pacific Coast for a time. Watts was building his version of the Georgian Bay Mackinaw at Vancouver. Gidley would have seen plenty of them in Ontario.

Captain William Watts Jr. credits Collingwood fishermen with opening up the fishing industry on Lake Winnipeg. The Collingwood boat yard shipped mackinaws to the Lake by rail. Watts felt the discovery of the fish stocks at Lake Winnipeg was due to the depletion of fish stocks in Lake Superior. He said "Even the Lake Superior was large and deep, it could not stand the strain put on it. It began to dwindle, until it became the survival of the fittest. The weaklings had to close shop. Then they discovered Lake Winnipeg. Well, we built boats for all the different lakes. [1]

With Collingwood fishermen, the brother of the company's founder Matthew Watts, and skiffs arriving by rail, Lake Winnipeg had plenty of Georgian Bay influence. "There were no boats on Lake Superior or Winnipeg, as understood as Upper Lakes, until the Collingwood fishermen went there to fish. I was there in 1880, and I saw for myself. There were Collingwood boats fishing in Lake Superior on the Canadian side in 1870." [2] Photographs of Lake Winnipeg's fishing fleet, particularly at Gimli, can easily be mistaken for Georgian Bay. Lapstrake, double ended clinker built fish boats line their shores. Even a small detail like a rubbing strake is identical to those turned out of the Collingwood Watts yard.

On the Pacific Coast, Watts & Trott's production of Columbia River skiffs in the same fashion as the Collingwood Skiff had a major impact on their fishing industry. Although designs were modified by other builders over the years, Watts feels that even Japanese

---

1. Captain William Watts Jr. to James Barry, September 15, 1937.
2. Captain William Watts Jr. to James Barry, September 8, 1938.

builders kept the same bow designs. Early images of fishing villages, like that at Steveston show collections of small craft with familiar hull designs.

Back in Ontario, Fishermen in Bronte at Lake Ontario received a train shipment of a handful of Watts-built fish boats. One boat is well documented, *Thistle*. Some note that two or three boats arrived in Bronte by rail. It would be likely that a few were shipped, it would have made more sense economically. Only after the arrival of the Collingwood model did other local builders start to duplicate their design.

Fishing boats at Gimli, Manitoba in 1926. These shapely craft show the influence of the classic Watts lines.
Photo: C.B.Donnely. National Archives of Canada PA20153

Hundreds, probably thousands of boats were constructed by William Watts and his descendants. Hundreds more sailed the lakes that looked like they were built by Watts. Watts didn't build every boat on the lakes, not by a long shot. Even a cursory glance through early photographs, post cards and drawings show countless, nameless, small craft that look strikingly like they were built by Watts, even if they weren't. Even today, some modern fibreglass row boats hearken back to designs resembling 150 year old models. Watts design characteristics were unique and their qualities as a boat were beyond compare, according to those who sailed them.

Tyrell was heading up a Geological Survey on Lake Winnipeg when he took this shot at Swampy Harbour in 1889. Fish boat Pterodactyl is at far left. The Collingwood firm of W. Watts & Sons had sent boats to the lake by rail.
Photo: J.B.Tyrell. National Archives of Canada PA50881

An Afternoon's Catch near Collingwood, Ont.

Recreational fishing in a motor launch at Collingwood. Watts Collection

"Back to the Camp" A Trip near Collingwood, Ont.

This postcard shows a launch near Collingwood. It resembles many of the Watts built launches, both in Collingwood and Vancouver. Watts Collection

Postcard showing a fishing village on Lake Superior.
Watts Collection

This square sterned, plumb bow, clinker built boat is being pulled ashore the south side of Great Slave Lake, North West Territories, 1899.
Robert Bell Collection, National Archives of Canada / C18876

186   W. WATTS & SONS BOAT BUILDERS

On the shores of Bronte, Ontario. Fish boats, showing the combination of sail and power. Net drying racks are scattered around the fish shacks. The shapely, lapstrake fish boat is square–sterned.
National Archives of Canada, PA84769

View of Manitowaning Bay, Manitoulin Island, Ontario. Watts Collection

Postcard illustrating a classic Mackinaw at Pointe au Baril. Watts Collection

W. WATTS & SONS BOAT BUILDERS

Maggie A was built for James Playfair by Morrill. She owes her lines to the Collingwood Skiff.
Huronia Museum Collection

A group of people 'simply messing around in boats' at Wasaga Beach, Ontario.
Watts Collection

The F.C. Watts, *owned by Stan Birch.*
Photo: Stan Birch, Watts Collection.

16 BUILDING THE F.C.WATTS

HULL 146 ½

"If I write another book, I'll include the story of Reg Watts... the thing I found so funny is those buddies of his, sitting around that pot bellied stove changing the plans, which ultimately dragged the project out for 30 years."

Bill Bramah, 1915–

The completion of a life-long dream, hobby or endeavour, while extremely rewarding, is in some ways anti-climactic. The fun and excitement is not in the end product, but in experiences, trials and adventures gained in getting there. Although it didn't start out that way, the thrill in building *F. C. Watts* was just that, the building. After her long–awaited launch, some 35 years after keel laying, the day-to-day escapades involved with her construction came to an end. A journey had ended.

Reg Watts took 35 years to construct the beautifully-proportioned steel sailing sloop, in sharp contrast to the few weeks his uncles took to construct similar vessels from wood. In Reg's defence, he also dealt with some 300 'consultants' eager to help him out. His uncles didn't have the benefit of that kind of help.

As a youth, exposure to a richer, more varied cross section of boat building knowledge may not have been possible, at least in the Collingwood area. This was just the environment that Reg Watts grew up with in this waterside town, on the shores of Nottawasaga Bay.

The *F. C. Watts* stands as a declaration of a colourful past and a dedication to a much–loved family. She is a glowing tribute to longevity and quality of design in boat building. Reg's home as a child was at 42 Maple Street, Collingwood. Maple Street then was a virtual who's-who of Collingwood's marine heritage. Florence McCall lived on Maple Street when Reg was a boy. Her family lived in a magnificent home formerly owned by Captain "Black" Pete Campbell.

"Maple Street at that time was a real marine community. Black Pete's grandson's widow, Mrs. Clainy Campbell, lived beside us with son Lorne, and the Fred Watts were next to them with 2 boys. Across the street from us the Captain Buntings had 2 girls and a boy. Farther up, Captain Montgomery had 3 boys–it was sad to learn that young John Montgomery hadn't made it back from World War II–he was such a lovely youngster. Then Ike Vankoughnet lived near Second Street, they had 3 girls. He had a fishing boat...We all played baseball after supper in the summer in the middle of the road, and after dark it was Red Light and Truth or Dare under the street light on Henderson's boulevard." [1]

Miss McCall later recalled "the only real excitement on Maple Street was when a farmer's young bull calf got loose and after throwing a man off his bike, ended up in the Captain Montgomery's yard. They were on vacation, and Captain Fred Watts put up a barricade of ladders to keep it in. We couldn't keep away, of course, so he lassoed it and secured it to the fence. A real rodeo on Maple Street!" [2]

Reg was named after Reginald Bassett, family friends and early settlers to the area. Always noted for his size and strength, Reg participated in the usual sports of hockey and baseball. He was an exceptionally strong swimmer and diver, like his brother Bill.

As a child growing up he would spend a lot of time at the boat shop. The shop of this time period, the 1920's and 30's, was very busy. The activity of the shop always drew a number of people. It was this social setting that was a strong magnet for Reg. Just the boat house was a draw. This was the place he learned to hold a hammer and to drive a nail. He played in the shavings on floor as a kid, and watched his uncles and father work. It was who he was. Pausing long enough, surely he could hear his mother calling him and his brother home for supper, "Bill, Reg, come on, it's getting cold!"

In winter, the sailors came home. The old salts would trudge through the deep, encrusted snow to help keep themselves aligned with stories of old, and share new tales from the season past. All would shed their trappings of trade and commerce, to gather around the pot belly stove and settle their feet among the wood shavings. Reminiscing took place as the boats were crafted around them. This setting became an irreplaceable wealth of knowledge for Reg to use in the building of the *F. C. Watts*

As Reg grew, he watched and learned. He absorbed a great deal of the area's history. It was an opportunity and a blessing most could only dream of having. Reg would grow and mature in the community as a student of King George School. He was an adventuresome youth. His log rolling and high–diving exploits were kept out of his father's ear shot. As a youngster, Reg worked on and off for his Uncle Matthew and his Father. During these years, he gathered and learned the necessary skills that would culminate in the *F. C. Watts*

Reg would follow his brother's footsteps for a period sailing on the lakes. He eventually found the time to court and marry Willa Wright of Wiarton. Reg wanted to marry Willa inside two months of their first meeting. Her parents made them wait six months. "That was the best day in my life, the day I met Reg," she said. "He was so funny.

1. McCall, Florence. Personal correspondence to Tracy Marsh, March 8, 1994.
2, McCall, Florence. Personal correspondence to Tracy Marsh, December 7, 1996.

A crew of workers at the Collingwood Shipyard. Standing at the back, left to right: Emerson (Fat) Wagner, Vic McDougall. Front row: Jamieson, Babe Scholtz, Reg Watts and Donald 'Nip' Spooner. Watts Collection

Two William Watts':
on the left, Bill Watts of Collingwood–son of Fred–shortly before his death in Montreal.
On the right, Capt. William Watts of Vancouver –son of William Watts of Collingwood. Watts Collection

Sometimes, when we were alone in the house, he would tell me stories that made me laugh so hard, I'd cry." [3]

After a few short months of marriage, war would break out. Reg enlisted in the Royal Canadian Navy, with postings in Halifax and Vancouver. After receiving an honourable discharge, Reg came back to Collingwood to his young family. This time Reg took up commercial fishing. He fished a year or two in the Lake Trout fishery with James 'Skip' Neville.

By this time, Reg's father had fallen ill with lung cancer. Reg worked in the Rigging Department at the Shipyard, where he stayed for 37 years. During his Shipyard years, with one building left from the original W. Watts & Sons operation, Reg would begin the construction of a boat that would be a life–long project.

From the same design of his father's last boat, *Navaid*, Reg began construction of a steel–hulled craft. Everything was there, just as if Reg's father had gone for the night.

The F.C.Watts *emerges from the boat house temporarily for sandblasting.* Watts Collection.

The tools were in place, the same tools that had served the Watts family since the 1850's. In this setting, Reg would begin a hobby that would take 35 years to complete.

This project would provide all the entertainment and frustration that comes in the construction of a large vessel.

3. Watts, Willa, interview May 26, 1994.

F. C. Watts *originally out of the shop. Reg Watts can be seen at the left hand side of the stern, guiding her out.* Watts Collection

Fred Watts' Navid. *Her molds were used by Fred's son Reg to construct* F. C. Watts. Navid *is on her way to Prescott, for use by the Department of Marine in 1948.* Watts Collection

Conversion of old family molds and templates that were once used in wooden boat construction began. Reg's boat would be of steel. Due to his father's business sense and Reg's access to the Shipyard–some of the large steel–shaping equipment was employed in its construction.

Reg would soon re-live the experiences he had as a child growing up in the boat shop. Now he was the seasoned story teller. The wood stove was there with the smell of freshly–cut wood. The personalities were there to gather around the stove and talk over politics, or their adventures as young children in Collingwood. From Shipyard workers to Shipyard managers, they all came. "There's always somebody in here," said Watts. They came to step back in time, visit and reminisce, with each giving his input on how the boat should be constructed. It was an environment in which Reg nurtured and flourished.

Reg's initial thoughts were to construct the vessel of wood, using the time–tested materials that his family had used before him. Why the choice was made is not clear. The wood was there and so was the steel.

The boat continued to evolve over the years of its careful

F. C. Watts completes the journey from the Watts boat house to the Collingwood Shipyard. Watts Collection

construction. All those passing through the doors of the boat house would give their opinion on what should be done next. From construction site to meeting place, the boat house became a home away from home. There was no rush to complete the job. The most pressing task each Saturday morning was to get the stove working and the shop heated before the guests arrived.

Many of the same names that Reg grew up with at the boat yard would return again a generation later, to witness the third generation of Watts boat building. Many participated in varying parts of construction, after all, they were shipbuilders. In fact, at some point the boat's construction would involve every department of the Shipyard. As the boat neared completion, many of the final changes may have been made to prolong the boat's stay in the old shop. His cohorts gathered after their shift, or even during, to check on the progress. Reg would pause to hear the different suggestions, look over newly–sketched plans and solve the problems of the world. "I must have about 300 helpers," Reg once pon-

The F. C.Watts *floats proudly in the water. Her builder Reg Watts is seen at the stern just after launching.* Watts Collection

dered. That's why it took so long. It was almost as if the lengthy discussions and suggestions for a little change here or there were stalling tactics. This place was too precious to lose. Once she was launched, it would be all over. Modifications provided Reg, and all those who entered in, a little more time to savour the years of memories over the duration of the boat's construction. Any time Reg was asked when the boat would finally hit the water, his typical response was "as soon as the water comes higher." There was no rush. Not all the time in the boat house was spent working. Reg confessed that some of his time was spent daydreaming. Sitting back in the old wicker chair, smoking a pipe, he was simultaneously looking back and looking ahead. Bill Bramah, an Ontario news personality, took a keen interest in Reg's work. Bramah, when commenting on the length of production, said "even Noah made better time."

When launch day came, it was a quiet affair. It was May 22, 1985. The crane operators and a few men to assist were all who were present. Unknown to Reg, a celebration had been planned. A regular shipyard-style christening for the vessel was arranged. Jack Bonwick, Human Resources Manager of the Shipyard, was the Master of Ceremonies. Shipyard workers, as well as office staff, all stood by to watch the boat hit the water for the first time. After three or four attempts to break the bottle on the bow proved fruitless, a little Shipyard ingenuity was employed. The boat was raised and lowered onto the bottle of bubbling champagne. The crush of the bottle welcomed the newly-christened *F. C. Watts*, named

to honour his father.

Cranes lifted the boat, setting her down in the waters of Collingwood harbour. *F. C. Watts* sat perfectly as hundreds of Watts boats had before her.

Over the course of the next year or two, Reg would make trips to the North Shore, Christian Island and several familiar stops around the Bay. Were these trips as rewarding as the ones Reg would have taken, as he sat in the well-worn captain's chair, fire crackling, contemplating his next project during the boat's construction? Whether rewarding or not, the trips were numbered.

Reg took sick in October of 1989, passing away in January 1990. Truly the end of an era.

F. C. Watts, which provided Reg with decades of enjoyment during its construction, would live on. The boat was eventually purchased by a retired dentist from Huntsville named Stan Birch. Stan modified the boat, changed the rigging and applied a fresh coat of paint to suit his needs. One thing Stan won't change is her name. *F.C. Watts* is still providing enjoyment for Stan and his family in the south seas.

A more fitting tribute to a family firm could not be had. A steel-hulled vessel with graceful lines, the solid *F. C. Watts* will remain a floating monument to almost a century and a half of boat building tradition on Canadian waters.

Reg Watts, builder of the F. C.Watts. Courtesy of Ursula Heller

GlossAry of terms

Aft refers to the stern area of a boat.

Aground boat has made contact with the bottom of a body of water, not enough water to float.

Amidships position between the bow and the stern, or between port and starboard sides, –middle of the boat.

Astern behind the boat.

Bail the act of removing water from the inside of a boat.

Ballast weight added to the inside of a boat to add stability.

Beam breadth or width of a boat.

Becalmed lack of wind, leaving a sail boat without a source of propulsion, excepting oars.

Bevel slope on an angle.

Bilge inside bottom of a hull below the waterline, or the curve of the sides toward the keel.

Boom spar which the foot or bottom of a sail is fastened.

Bow the front, or forward part of a boat.

Bowsprit a spar running from the bow of the boat, forward.

Forestays are fastened to the forward end.

Capsize boat turns completely over.

Carvel method of wooden boat construction. Planks are fastened on the ribs edge to edge, there is no overlapping. Sometimes referred to as smooth-skin.

Caulking driving cotton or oakum into seams of boat to prevent leaking, more common in carvel construction.

Centreboard a retractable keel made of wood or iron, usually amidships.

Charts maps of bodies of water indicating depths and shoals.

Clinker method of wooden boat construction. Planks overlap one another. Sometimes referred to as *lapstrake*.

Clipper bow style of bow which angles out from the bottom of the hull to the bow .

Cockpit undecked area of the top of a boat.

Cradle device used to keep boat upright when not afloat.

Crook portion of a tree that, because of their curvature, can be sawn out directly and used for such hull members as knees and stems.

Deck covered part of the top of a boat.

Draft depth of water necessary to float a boat.

Flitch pieces of live sawn lumber, with bark or natural edge still on the lumber.

Foot bottom of sail attached to boom.

Forestay wire rope running from bow to mast, sometimes referred to as headstay.

Forward position referring to area toward the bow.

Frames see *Ribs*.

Freeboard the portion of the side of a boat between the water-line and deck.

Garboard Strake strake or plank closest to the keel of the boat, the first to be affixed to the ribs.

Gunnel the upper edge, or side of a boat. Also referred to as *gunwale*.

Gunwale see *Gunnel*.

Halyard ropes and tackle used for lowering and raising sails.

Heel angle that a boat sails away from the straight vertical.

Helm tiller which controls the rudder.

Hull the body of a boat.

Jib small triangular sail carried forward of the mast.

Keel portion of the boat which extends below the hull.

Ketch two-masted boat with shorter mast aft.

Knee bracket used to secure seat of boat to the hull.

Lapstrake see *Clinker*.

Mackinaw a term used to describe a type of boat, usually double-ended, double-masted.

Main see *Mainsail*.

Mainsail the largest sail. Sometimes simply referred to as the main.

Mast vertical spar.

Oakum old rope-yarns teased out and tarred. Used for caulking purposes, hammered tightly into seams. Hot pitch, marine glue or lead paint is poured in to make seal seam.

Oar a pole with a blade end used for manually propelling a boat with leverage against the water.

Oar lock a U–shaped device used for holding oars and pivoting in place. Also referred to as rowlock.

Outrigger a projecting device fastened to the side or sides of a boat to prevent capsizing.

Plank see *Strake*.

Plumb straight vertical.

Port side the left side of a boat when looking forward.

Rib timbers which are perpendicular to the keel, either steamed or sawn in place, which determine the shape of the boat. Strakes are attached to the ribs. Also called *frames*.

Rig includes mast, sails and various lines used in their connection and operation.

Rudder device fastened to the stern of a boat which directs the course.

Sheer strake the top strake, or plank on a boat.

Shroud wire ropes which run from mast(s) to sides of boat to keep mast at a straight vertical.

Skeg the after part of the keel of the boat.

Skiff term used to describe a a variety of boats.

Spar refers to any pole, vertical or horizontal, on a boat.

Standing rigging permanent stays and shrouds, which support the masts and keep them upright.

Starboard side the right side of a boat looking forward.

Stay device used for attaching lines and ropes.

Stem the vertical portion at the exterior of the bow of a boat, to which all the strakes are attached.

Stern the back, or after part of a boat.

Stowage cargo area.

Strongback in boat building, any structure used to support keel while boat is under construction.

Strake another name for planks on a boat.

Thwart member running from port to starboard side of a boat, often used as a seat.

Tiller device which controls the rudder.

Topmast an additional portion added to the top of a mast.

Topsail small sail carried at the top of a mast.

Traveller metal rod to which the deck block of mainsheet attaches.

Wake disturbance of the water left behind as a boat moves through the water.

SELECTED BIBLIOGRAPHY

Publications

Arp, Barbara, ed. *Reflections, Collingwood an Historical Anthology.* Collingwood: Corporation of the Town of Collingwood, 1983.

Barcus, Frank. *Freshwater Fury.* Detroit: Wayne State University Press, 1986.

Barry, James P. *The Sixth Great Lake.* Toronto: Clarke-Irwin, 1978.

_____. *Georgian Bay, An Illustrated History.* Toronto: Stoddart Publishing, 1992.

_____. *Ships of the Great Lakes - 300 Years of Navigation.* Lansing: Thunder Bay Press, 1996.

Berchem, F.R. *The Yonge Street Story 1793 –1860.* National Heritage/Natural Historic Inc., 1996.

Campbell, William A. *Northeastern Georgian Bay and its People.* Sudbury: Author, n.d.

Gibson, Sally. *More Than an Island - A History of the Toronto Island.* Concord: Irwin Publishing, 1984.

Hamilton, James C. *The Georgian Bay.* 1873.

Hunter, Andrew F. *The History of Simcoe County. Barrie:* The Historical Committee of Simcoe County, 1909.

Knowles, Valerie. *Strangers at Our Gates - Canadian Immigration and Immigration Policy, 1540 - 1990.* Toronto: Dundurn Press, 1992.

Knuckle, Robert. *In the Line of Duty - The Honour Roll of the RCMP.* Burnstown: General Store Publishing House, 1994.

Leithead, Maggie. *Collingwood Skiffs & Side Launches, Building Canada's Marine Heritage.* Collingwood: The Collingwood Museum, 1994.

Lipke, Peter; Peter Spectre; Benjamin A.G. Fuller. *Boats, A Manual for their Documentation.* Mystic: Museum Small Craft Association, 1993.

Lunn, Janet and Christopher Moore. *The Story of Canada.* Toronto: Lester Publishing and Key Porter Books Ltd., 1992.

Marcil, Eileen Reid. *The Charley-Man - A History of Wooden Shipbuilding at Quebec 1763 - 1893.* Kingston: Quarry Press, 1995.

McCuaig, Ruth H. *Our Pointe au Baril.* Author, 1984.

Stacey, Duncan and Susan. *Salmonopolis: The Steveston Story.* Madeira Park: Harbour Publishing , 1994.

Thomas, Barry. *Building The Herreshoff Dinghy - The Manufacturers Method.* Connecticut: Mystic Seaport Museum Inc., 1993.

Turner, Ted and Gary Jobson. *The Racing Edge.* New York: Simon and Schuster, 1979.

Vassilopoulos, Peter. *Antiques Afloat, From the Golden Age of Boating in British Columbia.* Vancouver: Panorama Publications Ltd., 1980.

Government Documents

Canada. *Records of the Department of Militia and Defence, RG 9.*

Canada. *Records of the Department of Public Works, National Archives of Canada, RG 11.*

Canada. *Records of the Department of Transport, National Archives of Canada, RG 12.*

Canada. *Records of the Royal Canadian Mounted Police, RG 18.*

Canada. *Records of the Department of Fisheries and Oceans, RG 23.*

Canada. *Records of the Marine Branch, RG 42.*

Canada. *Records of the Geological Survey of Canada, RG 45.*

Collingwood, Town of. Assessment Rolls (various).

Census Return for Canada, 1861 and 1871.

Articles and Periodicals

Barry, James P. *Mackinaw Boats & Collingwood Skiffs.* Greenwich: Yachting Magazine, November 1940.

_____. *Huron and Haywood Boats.* Greenwich: Yachting Magazine, April 1942.

Joyce, Lorne. *Fish Boats in Sail. Inland Seas.* Vermillion: The Great Lakes Historical Society, Vol. 53 No. 1, Spring 1997.

Marsh, Tracy. *A Canadian Boat Building Legend, W. Watts & Sons family boat builders.* Brooklin: Wooden Boat Publications Inc. (No.130), May/June 1996.

McCannell, Captain James. *Shipping out of Collingwood.* Toronto: Ontario Historical Society Papers and Records, Vol. XXVIII 1932.

Snider, C. H. J. *Lake Fish boats Fished All Winter. Schooner Days DLXIII,* Toronto: The Evening Telegram, November 14, 1942.

_____. *Many Masts in Bronte. Schooner Days DCCCXXXIII.* Toronto: The Evening Telegram, February 7, 1948.

_____. *Fish boats Set Style for Yachts. Schooner Days DCCCXXXIX,* Toronto: The Evening Telegram, March 20, 1948.

ACKNOWLEDGMENTS

We had the good fortune to cross many paths during our research. Countless individuals helped us to learn a great deal. Many helped us with the generosity of their hospitality. Although each person or organization contributed in a different way, we are thankful for each and every act of kindness and trust, not to mention the time spent talking with us.

When the book was only a dream, James Barry, author of several books on Georgian Bay and the Great Lakes was a source of motivation. We are grateful for his encouragement and guidance throughout this process, which was new territory for us both. Lorne Joyce of Port Credit is probably one of the greatest sources of information on fish boats in sail in Ontario. He is an excellent historian, accentuated only by his memory for details that make the stories come to life. Betty Joyce made sure our multiple visits were well supplemented with delectable meals and treats. Henry N. Barkhausen of Jonesboro, Michigan kindly shared his stories about ordering and sailing his Watts built *Butcher Boy*. These three men actually owned or sailed in Watts built craft.

The Collingwood & District Historical Society helped to support our research with a generous donation. Our gratitude also goes to the Collingwood Public Library Board of Directors for their faith in our project, and Collingwood Municipal Council for endorsing the idea that our history is sought after and worth-while.

Early in our research we conducted a great deal of oral history interviews, which were all taped and transcribed to form a permanent record of our conversations. In every case, we were welcomed into people's homes, trusted with family photographs and provided with significant, and often humorous insights into the topic. We are thankful to George Kidd of Toronto for sharing his tales of sailing aboard *Nahma*; to Gordon 'Steamer' Clark of Collingwood for his perspective on boat building in Collingwood; James Keith of Collingwood for expressing the importance of a good boat in the life of a light keeper and his family; to Art and Brian Drever of Collingwood for one of the most memorable and laughter filled evenings we shared while exploring the life style of early fishermen and their tribulations; to Andrew Jardine of Collingwood for recalling working in the Collingwood shipwright's shop, formerly the Watts Boat Shop; Alan Richardson of Meaford for spending Good Friday with a couple of people who looked at practically every photograph in the corporate files; to Helen McIntyre of Mount Forest who has passed away since our interview, but gave us an insight into her family's work with Watts, beginning with her grandfather, Matthew Walton, sail maker; Pat Johnston of Parry Sound who persevered through our interview despite an incredible

storm and power interruption, to share the story of his father the light keeper, and the Watts boats they used; Art Oldfield of Collingwood told some amazing stories about boats and fishing around Thornbury and Pointe au Baril; George 'Bud' Akitt of Collingwood recalled his days under Fred Watts apprenticeship at the boat house; Chuck and Dorothy Parr of Collingwood entertained us for hours with their combined experiences with fishermen and Coast Guard operations; Marguerite 'Billy' Dance of Collingwood captured our hearts by sharing her experiences in her father's blacksmith shop that supplied the Watts Yard for a time; Walter White of Collingwood is now that community's only commercial fisherman, and he recalled his family roots fishing on the Bay, starting with boats from Watts; Scotty Carmichael of Collingwood told us of his relationship with the kids around Collingwood in his youth, including Bill and Reg Watts; John McIntyre of Guelph and John Walton of Collingwood trusted us with family photo albums; Ernie Brock of Collingwood vividly illustrated his experiences as an employee at the Watts Shop; Alan Haig-Brown of New Westminster, British Columbia who encouraged us to always write about what we loved; and Wentworth Walker of Toronto, and his cousin Barbara Heidenreich of Bailieboro who invited us to a splendid lunch to acquaint us with their family's love of *Nahma*; Marie Pearson who allowed us to marvel at the Watts built Patriarch on the Magnettewan River; Jim Trott of Collingwood for sharing information on his family and their connection with Watts; Earl and Jack McGauley of Stayner for sharing memories of the ship wright shop and Don Parrish of Collingwood who can recall details of people and places better than anybody; Ken Maxwell of Toronto who we dubbed the *Pequod* sleuth; Jim Kilgour for sharing stories and photographs of the Bay Belle ; to Nick Hunter of Florida for his excellent reproduction of the Walker family photographs and to Mark Adams of Orillia who has shared many tales about Ken Jones love affair with *Nahma*.

As a family story, many members of the Watts family were also important to our research. A few years ago, Mira (Watts) Conboy entertained an interview in New York, along with her children. In hindsight, we are thankful for her perspective on spending summers in Collingwood with her father's family. Her children and grand-children helped to facilitate this visit, and have answered no end of questions since to help with genealogical accuracy. Jack Watts of Langley, British Columbia was our chauffeur, tour guide and link to the West Coast. We could never begin to thank Jack for his hospitality and patience during the longest week on record. Bill Watts of White Rock, British Columbia was an important source of information on the operation and sale of The Vancouver Shipyard. Willa Watts of Collingwood, Peter's mother, has been patient and generous throughout the compilation of this book. Her living room and dining room was often converted into a library, archives and general think tank area. She too has shared some poignant tales that are now recorded for generations to come.

Although not related, Bill and Linda Watts of Sault Ste. Marie provided an unforgettable afternoon on their island at Pointe au Baril–Wattswood. In the midst of our work, they generously donated a Watts built life boat to The Collingwood Museum for preservation and exhibition. Their son Benjamin helped load the boat in the Sault for the journey home to Collingwood.

In the same token, Bill and Mary Bowler of the Owen Sound Marina helped to return *Pequod* back to the Watts Boat House by donating it with a view to restoring it.

Nick Hodson assisted with the history surrounding four generations of Watts as members of the Masonic Temple, Manito Lodge No. 90. Jerry Prager of Collingwood kindly loaned us some of his files on the *Asia*; Anita Miles of Ottawa helped out with some preliminary investigations at the National Archives; Conservator Steve Poulin of Toronto brought new life into photographs and paintings so they could be enjoyed here.

Rick Lair of Winnipeg, Manitoba who shared information about fishing at Gimli at a time when a great deal of the province was literally under water. Larry Crawford of Wyebridge gave us a marvellous tour of his shop and his Watts built lighthouse tender. Ken Holmes responded to a newspaper advertisement and contributed a charming photograph of his grandfather and his old fishing buddy in a Watts built row boat. We had many responses from individuals across the Nation. To each we are thankful, even if their contributions are not evident here, they may be used at some point in the future.

A number of professional heritage organizations were valuable resources for this publication. A significant collection of images used here hail from The Collingwood Museum. Many thanks go to Patricia Miscampbell, Assistant Curator, for her support and patience through the various stages of this work. Thanks also go to Carol Baum and Jackie Spafford of the Royal Ontario Museum; Pat Hamilton of the Huron County Museum; Barbara Ribey, Curator of the Bruce County Museum and Archives; Bruce Beacock, Archivist at Simcoe County Archives; George Cuthbertson and Margaret Brennan of the Royal Canadian Yacht Club; Garth Wilson, Curator of Marine and Fisheries; National Museum of Science and Technology; John Summers, Curator of The Marine Museum of Upper Canada; Glenn Wright, Staff Historian at the Historical Branch of the Royal Canadian Mounted Police; Roger Cole of the Nautical Research Guild; David Barron of Northern Shipwrecks Database; Michele Dale, Records Manager/Archivist of The Toronto Harbour Commissioners; Leonard McCann, Curator Emeritus and Joan Thornley, Curator of Collections of the Vancouver Maritime Museum; Mary Gazetas, Manager of Heritage Sites for the City of Richmond and the staff at Britannia Heritage Shipyards, Steveston, B.C.; Mary-Anne Nicholls, Archivist for The Anglican Diocese of Toronto; Lynn-Marie Richard, Curatorial Assistant at The Maritime Museum of the Atlantic in Halifax; Ray Marshall of the Irish Genealogical Society of Minnesota; Jamie Hunter and Bill Smith of the Huronia Museum in Midland; Freda McDonnell, Curator of The Meaford Museum and Kay McElwain of the Ship Registry Office in Vancouver. Staff at the Vancouver Archives and Vancouver Public Library provided delightful images. The staff of the National Archives of Canada are among the most patient and accommodating we encountered. Philip Gillesse of Ottawa, under contract with the National Museum of Science and Technology, provided skilful drawings of *Nahma* and her sail plan.

Robert 'Doc' and Joy Warne of Langley, British Columbia hosted us for an evening of Pacific Salmon and tours of the popular fishing grounds around Vancouver. Ursula Heller of Vancouver had the foresight to photograph the workers in the Collingwood Shipyard in the late 70's, we are thankful for her portrayal of Reg Watts in the Rigging Department. Murray Thompson of Collingwood helped us with video reproduction early in the project.

Anne Marsh Evans and Chris Fitzpatrick both lent their artistic talents to make the covers of the book come to life. Ronald MacRae should be given a medal for the patience and talent he provided in laying out this book. Much needed editing services were provided by Roger Hannon, and the text is better for his input.

In the early stages of our work, many authors and publishers provided moral and technical support. For this we thank John Dennison of Boston Mills Press in Erin and the crew at Lynx Images in Toronto, Andrea, Barbara and Russell.

While we hope to have included everyone who helped us out, we apologize for any omissions. Finally, without the love and encouragement of our families throughout 1997, we simply would not have been able to accomplish our goal.

INDEX

EΛΒOch 1936

Due in 1998

ONTARIO, SIMCOE & HURON RAILWAY

In 1855 the O.S & H. was considered the most important in the Dominion.

The authors Tracy Marsh and Peter Watts will chronicle the amazing story from conception to terminus.

The line ran from Toronto to Collingwood. It opened up growth in many communities along its route, while easing the opening of the Canadian West.